T0327317

The
Aimless Life

MUSIC, MINES, and REVOLUTION from the ROCKY MOUNTAINS to MEXICO

LEONARD WORCESTER JR.

*Introduced, Edited, and Annotated
by Andrew Offenburger*

University of Nebraska Press
LINCOLN

Published in Cooperation with the William P. Clements
Center for Southwest Studies, Southern Methodist University

Library of Congress Cataloging-in-Publication Data
Names: Worcester, Leonard, Jr., 1863–1939, author. | William
P. Clements Center for Southwest Studies. | Offenburger,
Andrew, editor.
Title: The aimless life: music, mines, and revolution from the
Rocky Mountains to Mexico / Leonard Worcester Jr.; intro-
duced, edited and annotated by Andrew Offenburger.
Description: Lincoln: University of Nebraska Press, [2021] |
"Published in cooperation with the William P. Clements Cen-
ter for Southwest Studies, Southern Methodist University." |
Includes bibliographical references and index.
Identifiers: LCCN 2020041059
ISBN 9781496222909 (paperback)
ISBN 9781496227744 (epub)
ISBN 9781496227751 (mobi)
ISBN 9781496227768 (pdf)
Subjects: LCSH: Worcester, Leonard, Jr., 1863–1939. | Mining
engineers—West (U.S.)—Biography. | Assayers—Colorado—
Leadville—Biography. | Assayers—Mexico—Chihuahua—
Biography. | Americans—Mexico—Chihuahua—Biography. |
Mineral industries—Mexico—Chihuahua—
History—Anecdotes. | Mexico—History—Revolution,
1910–1920—Personal narratives. | Mineral industries—West
(U.S.)—History—Anecdotes.
Classification: LCC TN140 .W67 2021
DDC 622.092 [B]—dc23
LC record available at https://lccn.loc.gov/2020041059

Set in New Baskerville ITC Pro by Laura Buis.

CONTENTS

ILLUSTRATIONS

MAJOR EVENTS IN THE LIFE
OF LEONARD WORCESTER JR.

Date	Event	Location
1860 (August 16)	Father Leonard (Sr.) and mother Mary Roche Spooner marry	Lee's Creek Mission, Cherokee Nation
1863 (August 26)	Born to Leonard (Sr.) and Mary Roche Spooner	Dayton, Kentucky
1868	Family moves	Tullahassee, Creek Nation
1871	Family moves	Cincinnati, Ohio
1873	Family moves	Greensburg, Indiana
1880	Father moves	Leadville, Colorado
1881	Rest of family moves	Leadville
1886	Travels with the GAR Juvenile Drum Corps	San Francisco
1887 (spring)	Joins Blue Ribbon Comedy Company; forms lasting relationships with the company players, including his future wife	Leadville
1887	Works for the Bancroft Company	San Francisco
1887	Travels with the GAR Juvenile Drum Corps	St. Louis, Missouri
1889 (May 22)	Marries Bernice Gertrude Beede	Leadville
1889	Moves to work for the Guggenheims	Pueblo, Colorado
1889 (October 7)	Son Herbert born	Pueblo

Date	Event	Location
1890	Moves	Leadville
1890 (August)	Travels with the GAR Juvenile Drum Corps	Boston
1891 (July 19)	Son Arthur W. born	Leadville
1893	Temporarily moves for mining work	Creede, Colorado
1893 (May 31)	Daughter Amy born	Leadville
1894	Teaches high school	Leadville
1896 (October 9)	Daughter Amy dies	Cripple Creek, Colorado
1897 (April 25)	Son Richard born	Cripple Creek
1900	Works as a mine manager	Cripple Creek
1900	Daughter Barbara born	Cripple Creek
1904 (May 15)	Mother dies	Leadville
1905	Works as an assayer	Cripple Creek
1905 (March)	Moves	Chihuahua, Mexico
1907	Sister Mabel dies	Leadville
1915 (February to March)	Imprisoned by Pancho Villa for allegedly not paying taxes on a shipment of ore	Chihuahua
1916 (January)	Witnesses casualties from the Santa Isabel Massacre	Chihuahua
1916 (January)	Moves north of the border; works for the remainder of his life based in El Paso but migrates between mine locations in Chihuahua, New Mexico, and Arizona	El Paso, Texas
1918 (March 22–23)	Attacked by Villa loyalists, purportedly led by Pablo López, while visiting mines	Chihuahua
1918–1930s	Manages and speculates in mines; employed by Robert Hamilton Bishop Jr.	Chihuahua, New Mexico, and Arizona
1932	Tours former work and family sites by car with Gertrude	Colorado
1939 (December 1)	Dies	El Paso
1949 (January 17)	Gertrude dies	El Paso

INTRODUCTION

IN EARLY MARCH 1915, NEWS BROKE IN EL PASO THAT Leonard Worcester Jr., a mining man in the border region, was being held in a Chihuahua jail "without trial or release on bond."[1] Worcester had been accused by officials loyal to Francisco "Pancho" Villa of defrauding a Mexican company, relating to a shipment of zinc, a charge without merit. Nevertheless, for all the difficulties he would have convincing Mexican officials of his innocence, Worcester equally struggled to prod American diplomats to intervene on his behalf. His wife, Gertrude, complained to her family that Secretary of State William Jennings Bryan had "absolutely no desire to protect or help us Americans or to know the truth," and that President Woodrow Wilson's special agent "passed through here, but did not investigate the case at all. He was dined and wined by the very people who are keeping my husband in jail. When I found out these things I had no hopes of help from that source."[2]

Thus emerged the Worcesters within a historical maelstrom of economic interests, foreign diplomacy, and revolution that had engulfed the U.S.-Mexican border region after 1910. Given his profession and nationality, Worcester was more likely than most to be caught up in international affairs. The region was tense, as American economic expansion clashed with an ascendant Mexican nationalism. For years he had worked as a leading assayer in Chihuahua, sampling minerals for purity, buying ores, and coordinating their exportation. Worcester was recognized as "learned and experienced in his profession which he has successfully followed for years and won a deserved and high reputation among mining men for proficiency, reliability and the prompt and careful attention he gives to all orders."[3] No amount of professionalism could save him from political realities, of course, but the pragmatism and measured response he displayed in a Chihuahua jail had served him well his entire life, from his birth in 1863 to his death in 1939, the year in which he wrote this memoir.

Born in the greater Cincinnati region during the Civil War, Worcester matured in a pivotal era. In the year before his birth, the United States passed three pieces of legislation that would chart the nation's future through western expansion. The Homestead Act, Pacific Railway Act, and Morrill Act systematized private land acquisition, connected the Far West by rail, and ensured agricultural research and public higher education, respectively. These acts enabled families of modest means, like the Worcesters, to seek a brighter future beyond the Ohio and Mississippi Rivers. The common hope for a better future, held by countless settlers and squatters, came at the expense of indigenous peoples. American dreams became possible only with a militarized federal government, clearing lands long claimed by Native American sovereign peoples. As a result, the greater Ohio region of Worcester's birth was undergoing tremendous change. Marked by regional tensions before the Civil War, and shaped by western migration thereafter, the Middle West shifted along with the nation's orientation further West.

One can sense this transition in Worcester's memoir, when, early in the boy's life, his family moved to the Creek Reservation in present-day Oklahoma and back within two years. For their departure, the family traveled by steamer along the Ohio River and other waterways, completing the journey overland by carriage. Upon their return, the Worcesters rode the Ohio & Mississippi Railroad, watching behind them as men changed its tracks from six-foot to standard gauge. Standardized rails were replacing water routes in the West as the nation's most cost-effective transportation network.

Beyond geography and chronology, one could make a strong argument that the Worcesters personally symbolized, more than most, these succeeding Euro-American generations of western expansion. His distant paternal English (and New England) roots had grown for centuries in American soil. Most notably, his grandfather, the missionary Samuel Austin Worcester, bestowed national and historical import to the family name. He, of course, played a significant role in working with the Cherokee: to translate the Bible, to create the first Native American newspaper, and, as political pressures mounted under the administration of Andrew Jackson, to resist the tribe's removal. His imprisonment for refusing to relinquish lands to regional squatters, and his subsequent victory in the Supreme Court case *Worcester v. Georgia* (1832), was nevertheless but a pause in the push for removal along the infamous Trail of Tears. Samuel's son, Leonard Worcester's father (Senior), also worked as a missionary before switching to alternate careers of a settler colonist: directing choirs and selling musical instruments, books, and paper products, among others. Within the span of three paternal generations, then, from Samuel to Leonard Jr., the Worcester men had migrated away from lives that connected directly to Native American affairs, and toward a migratory, itinerant professionalism determined by available opportunities and the nation's economy.

Worcester's maternal ancestry is comparatively lesser known, unfortunately. Descendants today recognize the centrality of education to his mother, Mary Roche Spooner. Born in Cincinnati (1834), after turning eighteen she served as a missionary to the Dakota Indians in Minnesota Territory for a period of two years.[4] She then returned to Ohio to earn a degree from Western Female Seminary (now Miami University) in 1858. Soon thereafter, she left to work as a teacher on Cherokee Nation lands, where she met Leonard Worcester Sr., later marrying him at Lee's Creek Mission in 1860.[5]

Within the life of Worcester Jr. one can see the influence of these preceding generations. He forever remained a resolute Presbyterian, influenced by both parents' commitment to missionize Native Americans. After boyhood he participated in musical and theatrical endeavors, and persevered through pragmatic professionalism. He pursued a series of disparate professions from Indiana to Colorado, California, Texas, Chihuahua, New Mexico, and Arizona: as a druggist, musician, drum corps leader, piano tuner, and high school teacher before embarking upon a career assaying minerals, operating ore hoists, running cars, and managing mines. Opportunities for employment and an earnest work ethic—far from any sense of manifest destiny—guided Worcester throughout the borderlands and in his life.

For this reason, drama ran anathema to this jack-of-all-trades. He took in stride and without panic the emergency of being jailed by Pancho Villa in 1915, much like his onetime chance participation in the Cripple Creek strike of 1894. Such dramatic and historically important moments contrasted acutely with Worcester's view of himself and of his "aimless" life. Beginning his memoir, he promises little more than the "drab" and "plain tale" of an "ordinary" American of "average intelligence and education."[6] Setting aside the flashpoints of imprisonment and the labor strike, in a way Worcester is right. His life generally lacked the excitement generated by other, more colorful characters during the Gilded Age and Progressive Era. He did not destroy saloons with hatchets in the name of prohibition, à la Carry A. Nation. He did not rouse Americans with the thunderous oratory of Bryan's Cross of Gold speech. He did not charge up San Juan Hill. The active verbs "destroy," "rouse," and "charge" may have characterized his era, but Worcester was a linking-verb man, more Prufrock than Pershing. He mined properties in formal attire, ever the Presbyterian American who measured success by the carload of ore.

This steadfastness, this ordinariness, this "aimless life" therefore ran counter to an era defined by manifest destiny and the bombast of boosterism. Indeed, throughout his memoir Worcester seems betrayed by lofty dreams, implicitly lamenting never having struck the mother lode. Writing in his last year of life, he had a view of its full trajectory. However taciturn the narrator may seem in the second half of the narrative, readers should note that the mining man, when compared to others struggling through the Great Depression, managed to provide a quite comfortable life for himself and for his family.[7] Any disillusionment of Worcester's must therefore be allayed with the relative success he achieved in a place and time in which starvation and migration determined the fates of many.

While his memoir seems to apologize for not providing the heart-pounding thrill of war, historians of the American West will find it valuable for several reasons. The everyday nature of his life, in fact, offers unique historical value and, paradoxically, makes his narrative compelling. His descriptions of childhood in the Midwest and the Colorado region will appeal to scholars tracking the influence of nuclear families in mining regions. Worcester's experiences—largely connected to his family, their church, and his father's music and stationery store—offers a counterpoint to Elliott West's characterization that boys "found jobs that took them away from the influence of home," and that they "often seemed to take on the acquisitive, aggressive, economically individualistic values characteristic of the mining frontier."[8] Likewise, historians of mining will find a new, fresh voice detailing operations from Colorado to Chihuahua. Worcester's comments are insightful, for example, on his approaches to safety while operating a hoist, on (his opinion of) the superiority of Cornish miners, on the routinization of work, on the ease of floating from one job to the other, and on the direct link between national economic crises and their immediate effects underground.

Scholars of music will note lives shaped by sound. Today we tend to see circuits of professionalism (e.g., vaudeville) separating singers from assayers, but the lives of Worcester, of his wife and children, and of his parents remind us that many folks in the Midwest, Far West, and the borderlands benefitted from music as a part-time passion or temporary fix. Worcester's involvement with the Grand Army of the Republic Juvenile Drums Corps, shaped by his father's service as bandmaster during the Civil War, is a case in point, as he traveled from Colorado to San Francisco, St. Louis, Washington DC, and Boston for annual performances and self-employment. His memoirs convey the pride he took in performative excellence, as does a clipping from the *Boston Globe* in 1890: "Among the crack drum corps now in town with the veterans, are [Worcester's] Leadville, Col., boys," who were "anxious to meet other visiting drum corps in a competitive drill."[9] Worcester became actively involved in the theatrical and musical scene in Leadville and greater Colorado after 1887, when he participated in productions by the "Blue Ribbon Comedy Company" and with performances at church. He references the company often throughout his memoir, evidence that the social relations facilitated by music had a profound impact on his personal life.

Borderlands historians will value Worcester's voice for its discussion of the Mexican Revolution. Memoirs, of course, can fall prey to romanticism, nostalgia, or personal glorification, all of which increase when related to revolution. And some of Worcester's narrative comes as second-hand knowledge, e.g., his telling of the Santa Isabel Massacre. What he *can* offer, though, are views into the everyday routines of life and work in revolutionary Chihuahua, detailed descriptions of confinement in 1915, and evidence as to contemporary interpretations of what was then called "the Mexican situation." His work in the Mexican North continued unimpeded despite outbursts of conflict and violence, and he often migrated between El Paso, where his family was based, and mining claims throughout Chihuahua, New Mexico, and Arizona. Through this offering Worcester's manuscript joins a multitude of other memoirs of Americans on the ground. Its matter-of-fact authorship by a mining and business man, however, makes it rare and historically valuable.

These strengths and historical contributions have carried Worcester's story from the inked hammers of his typewriter in

1939 to the pages in your hands today. Yet it contains significant weaknesses that raise questions to be addressed and, if used the classroom, to be discussed. Most importantly: *where are the women?* Based solely on this text, Worcester dismisses women professionally and ignores their influence personally. In Cripple Creek, he offered poor investment advice to an unnamed woman, whose husband berated him after the funds plummeted to zero. As a result, he tells readers, he has "shunned business with women ever since." In his personal life, his wife, Gertrude, passes without much mention and without a name. His wedding appears as an introductory clause to professional pursuits: "So when I got married in 1889, I went to Denver on my honeymoon, and secured a job in the repair shop of the music company."

Gertrude (Beatrice Gertrude Beede) was born near the shores of Lake Erie in Lenox, Ohio, on June 14, 1868. A year after her mother died in 1874, she and her brother, George Owen, accompanied their father, Moses, and his in-laws to Colorado on a "sojourn . . . for the benefit of his health." By 1877, Moses had remarried and suffered a setback when his mill in Ohio burned. He then returned to the Middle West and led an active civic life. Gertrude and her brother likely had childhoods marked by migration between Leadville and Ohio. One source suggests she, "a gifted musician," graduated from the New Lyme Institute near Lenox, while the 1880 federal census recorded her and her brother in the care of their aunt and uncle in Leadville. It is clear, though, that by the latter 1880s, Gertrude—now twenty years old—began making a name for herself in the music and theater scene in Leadville, where she met Worcester and fell in love.[10] They would spend the next fifty years together, until his death ten years prior to hers, giving birth to and raising Herbert (1889–1947), Arthur (1891–1956), Amy (1893–96), Richard (1897–1975), and Barbara (1900–1978).

What to make of such dismissal and general lack of family life in a memoir? The silence is all the more profound when one considers the provenance of the manuscript: passed down through successive generations of daughters, and encircled with the research notes and questions of his granddaughter. The standard response for skewed views or representations of gender and race—"that's what it was like back then"—fails to account for more complicated dynamics at work here, though Worcester, it seems, did ascribe to paternalistic biases against women in the workforce. This is not surprising, especially considering his trade in the male-dominated mining industry. We can also infer from this that Worcester was writing not for his family but for a male readership interested in history—battles, strikes, and so forth—which also explains his apologetic first paragraph. He therefore has anticipated his readers' interests and tailored his life to fit those expectations as well as possible. This approach silences his home life, unfortunately, such that he does not mention the death of his three-year-old daughter, Amy, from typhoid fever in 1896.

Absences from this narrative, however, do not correlate with inactivity. Photographs capture doting parents in Chihuahua. Letters between a father and sons suggest paternal care and mutual professional interests. Social notes and articles from El Paso newspapers reveal a family participating frequently in the city's social events. More often than not, this involved performing music for church activities and local gatherings. Gertrude, for her part, was well read and taught piano lessons, while their daughter, Barbara Worcester Holm, became an active proponent of progressive organizations like the League of Women Voters, Planned Parenthood, the Red Cross, and the YMCA. Sons Herbert and Richard worked as electrical engineers, while Arthur speculated in mine development.

Less evidence remains to uncover the family dynamics undiscussed in Worcester's writing, but we can get a general idea from Barbara Holm Coleman, his granddaughter, who passed away in December 2020 at ninety-three years of age and who had limited direct knowledge of his immediate family. In January 2019 I conducted an oral history interview with Coleman at her home in Dallas, accompanied by her daughter Anne Worcester Coleman Rowe. Coleman recalled some memories of her grandparents, though she was merely twelve years old when her grandfather died. Some moments remained etched in her mind, firm and consistent, despite the passage of time. Her strongest recollections of her grandfather included watching him work at a roll-top desk in his home office, and observing a moment of passion, when his soft-spoken nature broke. In an argument with his son-in-law of Scottish ancestry, Leonard Jr. guffawed at an assault on the English Crown: "Nevertheless," she recalled him thundering, "Queen Victoria was a wonderful woman!" Chuckling at the memory, Coleman concluded, "It was unusual for him to get that angry." The anecdote reveals how Leonard Jr., like many Americans, strongly claimed his ancestry while celebrating his American citizenship.

Regarding marriage and gender dynamics within the household, his granddaughter also recalled a general separation of duties common to the time—Leonard providing the income from his employment, and Gertrude managing household affairs—and that Leonard frequently went prospecting along the Turquoise Trail in New Mexico. The couple may have led compartmentalized lives to a certain extent, but they shared strong beliefs in the universal importance of higher education. "Education and admiration for being well educated was my heritage," she said. Evidence of this exists in family pictures and surviving books, handed down through generations, "about music theory, music history, opera, symphonies, [and] classical music."[11]

Worcester's granddaughter did discuss one important anecdote absent from the memoir: that Leonard and Gertrude and their four children, when they fled north to El Paso due to the intensifying Mexican Revolution, took with them from Chihuahua an orphaned girl, Marina, who later moved to a "Mexican neighborhood" of El Paso and continued to work as a domestic servant for the family. Coleman spoke of Marina as a trusted and beloved servant who kept a copy of the housekey. One reference to Marina exists in a letter held by descendants, but beyond this fleeting snippet, her identity could not be confirmed in any border-crossing documents or other archival records. Coleman spoke fondly of her and described in great detail Marina's involvement with the family.[12] The documentary silence paradoxically speaks loudly about the erasure of Mexican Americans, and of the vectors of race and migration, along the border. It is my hope that the publication of this memoir may lead to identifying Marina and her descendants, and to understanding their own position in this transnational story.

While Coleman was an imperfect source for insight into the family, given the limitations of age, she was our only one to fill an ever-present gap in the manuscript. Her observations, interpretations, and recollections of events from eighty years ago add data points to an elusive historical narrative. Without additional voices, we can only speculate as to how her thoughts connect to the memoir Worcester left behind. It is incomplete, yes: lacking description of family life, and missing a page.[13] As with his granddaughter's partial memories, though, readers must accept the limitations of what Worcester offers. From this perspective, *The Aimless Life* adds an important voice into a robust chorus of first-person memoirs in the American West and its borderlands. Worcester gives us a reflection on life and work, written by a multiskilled migratory white man, one who establishes himself as a mining authority in the borderlands at a critical point in time for intracontinental relations. He chronologically follows a deep tradition of more renowned autobiographers and memoirists who speak to their own Wests and borderlands, for example: Black Hawk on Sac and Fox removal from the western Illinois region after 1830, Dame Shirley on life in the mining camps of midcentury California, Black Elk on the experience of Plains Indians after 1880, and Ernesto Galarza on growing up in California in the early 1900s, among many others.[14]

Worcester makes two unique contributions to this tradition. First, he offers an on-the-ground perspective of American economic expansion into Mexico. Between 1880 and 1920 individuals and companies migrated south into Mexico with the extension of railroad networks. Aggressive prospectors, dreamers, and capitalists south of the border repeated a pattern familiar to the American West, but this movement also exacerbated tensions among Mexican social classes. Though investment successes were hit-and-miss before 1910, the outbreak of the Mexican Revolution pushed back against U.S. economic expansion, forcing many miners, missionaries, exiles, and a few farmers back north of the border. Worcester fully traveled along this historical path as he prospected and managed mines between Colorado and Chihuahua before 1916, and then worked in the region while based in El Paso thereafter.

His recollections of revolutionary Mexico, describing an insurgency frequently unsettling his work in Chihuahua, adds to a substantial list of American memoirists south of the border, including journalists, missionaries, colonists, and capitalists.[15] Worcester is to reporting on borderland mining what John Reed was to documenting Pancho Villa's rebellion in *Insurgent Mexico*.[16] A particularly fruitful comparison, though, can be made with the life and work of Luella and Irving Herr, the latter another mining engineer whose family resided in Guanajuato from 1910 to 1932. Worcester and Herr share similarities for their profession, but their different source bases (single-line diary entries in the case of the Herrs, supplemented with media reports and letters, and a memoir for Worcester) and their separate locations combine to show the variations of revolutionary Mexico.[17]

Second, his memoir reveals the ease by which Anglo-Saxon, American-born men could travel the West, following new opportunities based on social mobility. The facility to further the goals of capitalist expansion enabled Worcester to be, like hundreds of thousands of other western migrants, an agent of displacement and conquest. This "empire of innocence" forged the continental United States.[18] We cannot criticize someone for wishing to better his social positioning by changing professions in another region, by prospecting for potential wealth, or by providing a more comfortable life for his family, but we readers can be cognizant of how the smooth ride of settlers and capitalists into the West was, for others, a turbulent, life-changing, or fatal enterprise. Nothing illustrates this better than the brief transformation of experiences in dealing with Native Americans between Worcester's famous grandfather, who fought against dispossession of the Cherokee, and our narrator here, who barely recognizes in this memoir any indigenous presence beyond his boyhood on Creek lands in Indian Territory. And there is ample other evidence: his being called a racial epithet when, as a young boy, he spoke with a Southern accent, and his ability to escape this characterization and later benefit from a privileged position of social mobility.

This privilege in part accounts for why I consider Worcester's life an example of American western expansion as much as one of borderland business. The mining man certainly spent the majority of his professional life along the Colorado-Chihuahua corridor, overseeing the shipment of ore from Mexico and the West to eastern markets. To interpret *The Aimless Life* exclusively as a borderland memoir, though, would be to go against the very strengths of that methodology. Studies employing the borderlands model excel at explaining migratory lives, uncovering subaltern and/or indigenous histories otherwise on the margins of, or absent from, grand narratives. "If frontiers were the places where we once told our master American narratives," Pekka Hämäläinen and Samuel Truett have argued, "then borderlands are the places where those narratives come unraveled."[19] Might a scholar use a borderlands approach to analyze the Camp Grant Massacre, narrated from the perspective of multiple peoples? Absolutely. To address American capital, cross-border Mexican labor, and racial division? Yes.[20] But pigeonholing this memoir as a borderlands document, about a successful mine manager and businessman in the El Paso–Chihuahua region, felt like misappropriating a methodology best reserved for challenging nationalist histories. Nevertheless, a strong case to the contrary can be made.

This raises an important question that scholars have yet to fully discuss: is a borderland framework *appropriate* for historical actors in privileged positions? The life of Worcester implicitly raises this question. Despite its flaws and its notable silences, *The Aimless Life* makes a significant contribution to the history of American industrial expansion and the U.S.-Mexican borderlands, allowing us to hear the voice of a pragmatic man crossing professional, temporal, and national boundaries.

Origin of the Manuscript and Its Editing

At least two drafts of the memoir were typed, with one lost over the years. The surviving typescript draft is represented in the pages that follow. According to Worcester's great-granddaughter, Anne Worcester Coleman Rowe, the memoir passed from Leonard Jr. to his wife, and then to succeeding generations of daughters: first to his only surviving daughter, Barbara Worcester Holm, and then to Coleman and to Rowe.[21]

In 2000 Rowe originally approached Texas Western Press to publish the memoir, which put her in touch with Dr. James M. Day, Emeritus Professor of English at the University of Texas at El Paso, who worked on editing the manuscript until his death in 2005. After Dr. Day's passing, the original manuscript lay in wait until 2017, when Rowe renewed efforts to pursue its publication, eventually connecting with the Clements Center for Southwest Studies at Southern Methodist University. The Clements Center then introduced Rowe to me, a former postdoctoral fellow with research experience related to Americans in the Mexican North, and to her great-grandfather's "Aimless Life." Appropriately, she and I first met at the Western History Association annual conference in San Antonio in 2018. I chose not to consult Dr. Day's previous work on the manuscript, to avoid any interpretive influence.

In its original typescript form, Worcester's memoir can test readers' patience. At the beginning, one senses him striving to overcome his self-perception as a drab subject. The opening paragraph contains lyrical phrasing and, as such, prepares the reader for a crafted narrative about an Everyman experience in the American West. By page five, though, Worcester abandons any pretense to literary flair and heaves upon the reader the rest of the memoir, all 115 pages, in a single paragraph! Other quirks of style abound, in particular the overuse of "so" to link one event with another ("So I decided to take any job at the smelter"). In an effort to improve readability, while retaining the unadorned voice of a miner in the borderlands, I made three significant adjustments. First, I very rarely inserted or removed words to improve readability or clarify Worcester's intentions. Only in cases where the change constituted a substantial edit, in my opinion, did I bracket the text. Otherwise I erred on the side of narrative flow. Second, I broke up the narrative into paragraphs by identifying topic sentences as much as possible. And third, I divided the memoir into six chapters. A timeline has been added based on the memoir and on supplementary research.

Throughout the process of preparing this for publication, I conducted research to verify Worcester's claims and to test his accuracy. With a few minor exceptions, his memoir proved impressively accurate. Where his memory did fail him, I have either corrected the mistake in brackets (e.g., misidentifying a person) or left the error and provided a clarifying footnote (e.g., a date off by a year). After test-sampling Worcester's claims in dozens of instances, and finding that the historical record coincided with his narrative, I am confident his pages were written earnestly and without exaggeration. It is neither perfect nor complete, but Worcester's memoir contributes significantly to our understanding of the mining and musical Wests he experienced, and to the revolutionary borderlands his family called home.

Notes

1. "Worcester Is Innocent, Says Mining Firm Official," *El Paso Herald*, March 3, 1915, 3.

2. "Angeles Slated to Be President," *Marion Daily Star*, March 24, 1915, 2.

3. "Chihuahua, the Metropolis of Northern Mexico," *El Paso Herald*, July 1, 1908, 11.

4. Spooner and her sister, Lucy, were recruited by their cousin, Moses Adams, who had been associated with the Lac qui Parle Mission. Jon Willand, "Lac qui Parle and the Dakota Mission" (Madison MN: Lac Qui Parle County Historical Society, 1964), 215.

5. "A Tableau of the families, and single persons, connected with the American Board of Commissioners for Foreign Mission in the Dakota Mission, during the quar-

ter of a century 1835–1860, with the boarding scholars," Stephen R. Riggs and Family Papers, Minnesota Historical Society; Worcester Family Bible, private holdings of Anne Worcester Coleman Rowe, Dallas, Texas.

6. Worcester means "native born."

7. In one of Worcester's financial registries, which he used to manage mining expenses, his salary is documented as $200/month through the worst of the Great Depression, an income 50 percent higher than the U.S. average.

8. Elliott West, "Heathens and Angels: Childhood in the Rocky Mountain Mining Towns," *Western Historical Quarterly* 14, no. 2 (April 1983), 148. See also West, *Growing Up with the Country: Childhood on the Far Western Frontier* (Albuquerque: University of New Mexico Press, 1989).

9. "Wants to Show Itself," *Boston Globe*, August 14, 1890, 9.

10. *Biographical History of Northeastern Ohio, Embracing the Counties of Ashtabula, Geauga and Lake* (Chicago: Lewis, 1893), 292. Moses, George Owen, and Gertrude traveled with their late matriarch's sister, Mary, and her husband, George Henderson; Harriet Taylor Upton, *History of the Western Reserve, vol. II* (Chicago: Lewis, 1910), 1239; [M. W. Beede], "How Leadville Received Name," *Herald Democrat*, July 28, 1914, 2.

11. Correspondence with Anne Worcester Coleman Rowe, March 12, 2020.

12. Coleman believes that Marina died after 1971, and she recalled attending the funeral in El Paso with her mother. The only potentially identifying detail she could remember was that Marina's oldest son attained the rank of captain in the Army, likely stationed at Fort Bliss. An inquiry to Fort Bliss did not return helpful information in this regard.

13. The original typescript pages of *The Aimless Life* are double-spaced, but they are missing a page (identified as such in this published version). This typescript also contains an extra single-spaced page from another (lost) draft of the memoir. Unfortunately, the content on the single-spaced page does not fill in gaps from the missing page of the extant copy, but comparing the text does make it clear that the lost copy was an earlier and rougher draft.

14. Donald Jackson, ed., *Black Hawk: An Autobiography* (Champaign: University of Illinois Press, 1964); Louise Marlene Smith-Baranzini, *The Shirley Letters from the California Mines, 1851–1852* (Berkeley: Heyday, 2001); John G. Neihardt, *Black Elk Speaks: The Complete Edition* (Lincoln: University of Nebraska Press, 2014); Ernesto Galarza, *Barrio Boy* (Notre Dame: University of Notre Dame Press, 1971).

15. Examples include John Reed, *Insurgent Mexico* (New York: Appleton, 1914); James D. Eaton, *Life Under Two Flags* (New York: Barnes, 1922); Thomas Cottam Romney, *Mormon Colonies in Mexico* (Salt Lake City: University of Utah Press, 2005); and Henry Raup Wagner, *Bullion to Books: Fifty Years of Business and Pleasure* (Los Angeles: The Zamorano Club, 1942). See also the scholarly work by Timothy J. Henderson, *The Worm in the Wheat: Rosalie Evans and Agrarian Struggle in the Puebla-Tlaxcala Valley of Mexico, 1906–1927* (Durham: Duke University Press, 1998).

16. Reed, *Insurgent Mexico*.

17. Robert Woodmansee Herr and Richard Herr, *An American Family in the Mexican Revolution* (Wilmington DE: S.R. Books, 1999).

18. On the "empire of innocence," see Patricia Nelson Limerick, *Legacy of Conquest: The Unbroken Past of the American West* (New York: Norton, 1987), chap. 1.

19. Pekka Hämäläinen and Samuel Truett, "On Borderlands," *The Journal of American History* 98, no. 2 (September 2011), 338.

20. The field of borderland studies is robust. In these two examples, I refer to Karl Jacoby, *Shadows at Dawn: A Borderlands Massacre and the Violence of History* (New York: Penguin, 2008); and Katherine Benton-Cohen, *Borderline Americans: Racial Division and Labor War in the Arizona Borderlands* (Cambridge: Harvard University Press, 2009).

21. Email with Anne Worcester Coleman Rowe, September 19, 2018.

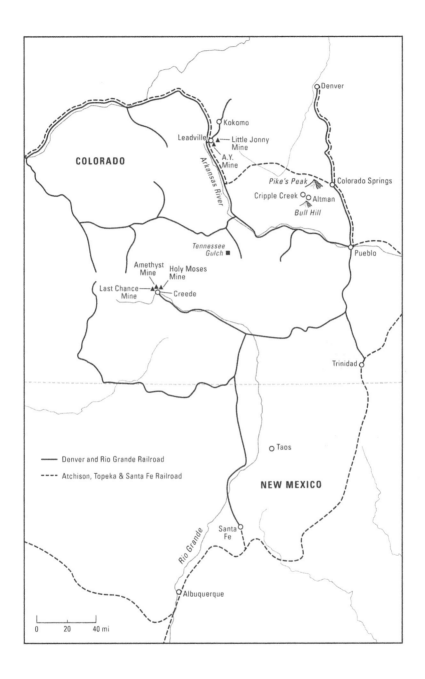

1. Map of principal locations in the life of Leonard Worcester Jr., 1880–1905.
Created by Erin Greb.

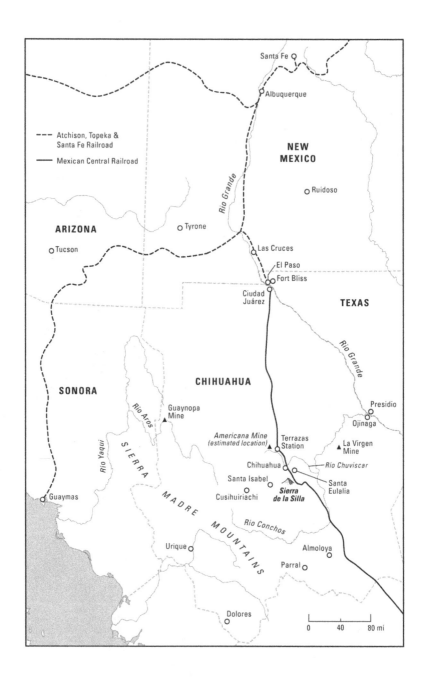

2. Map of principal locations in the life of Leonard Worcester Jr., 1905–39.
Created by Erin Greb.

The
Aimless Life

1

Childhood and American Transformations, 1863–1881

THIS IS THE PLAIN TALE OF THE LONG LIFE OF AN ORDI-
nary native-born American of average intelligence and education, without special talent or unusual opportunity, never
rich, never in actual want, never holding any important position politically, economically, or socially. Surely a drab and
uninteresting recital, especially as the writer has neither literary talent nor experience, a commonplace person with only
commonplace thoughts and modes of expression. But most
of our interest seems to center about the daily happenings
of our ourselves and our neighbors, and when we meet our
talk is principally of such things. So who can tell, perhaps it
may seem interesting to some. I am going to write it anyhow,
and, if it interests no one, there is no harm done. Perhaps as I
progress practice may improve my style so that it may become
interesting.[1]

My father was born in the Indian Territory in 1836, son of a
Yankee missionary to the Cherokee Indians, who that same year
established the first printing press in what is now Oklahoma.[2]
To complete his education my father was sent to the Academy
at St. Johnsbury, Vermont, where, during vacations, he worked
in the scale factory of the Fairbanks Brothers and learned the
machinist's trade.[3] Then he married and went to Van Buren,
Arkansas, to teach music. But soon the Civil War started, and
he took his wife to live with her mother in Dayton, Kentucky,
until the war should be over.[4]

My mother was born at Cincinnati, Ohio, the daughter of pioneers from New Hampshire, who came down the Ohio River on a flat-boat from Pittsburgh to Fort Washington, afterwards named Cincinnati, with all their belongings aboard. Her father took up two homesteads, one at Fort Washington, the other up the river a little way, on the Kentucky side, and he built the first brick house in Cincinnati, a two-story one on the river bank. My mother was born and grew up on the farm and became well acquainted with the Beecher family, as the farm adjoined the Lane Theological Seminary, of which the President was Dr. Lyman Beecher, father of Henry Ward Beecher and Harriet Beecher Stowe. My mother used to tell me tales of the eccentricities of Dr. Beecher, which were current during her girlhood. She graduated from the Western Female Seminary at Oxford, Ohio, and in that little graduating class was a daughter of Salmon P. Chase and a girl who was afterward the wife of President Benjamin Harrison.[5] As soon as she graduated, she went as a missionary to the Sioux Indians in Dakota, and was later transferred to the Indian Territory, where she was married.[6]

I was born in 1863 in Dayton, Kentucky, across the river from the eastern end of Cincinnati, in a two-story frame house at Goose Corner, about a hundred yards from the high vertical river bank. My father bought this house when it became apparent that the war would last a long time, and my mother would have to stay in Dayton while he went to the war. Goose Corner was so called because it was a gathering place for geese. Dayton was peopled almost entirely by immigrants from Saxony and their children, who spoke German, wore wooden shoes, ate black bread, drank much beer, which German brewers made in Cincinnati, and kept many geese and goats, which roamed the dusty streets and invaded the gardens when the gates were left open or the goats could jump the fences. One could always tell who was at home by the wooden shoes on the doorstep. The maker of the wooden shoes lived near us, and I was much interested in watching him carve out a pair of shoes from two blocks of basswood in just a little while, with a few crude tools.

The price was twenty-five cents a pair. These people were industrious, thrifty, god-fearing folks, Catholics who maintained a big red-brick church with a tall steeple, stained glass windows, a pipe organ, and a German priest.

That river bank was about forty feet high, vertical, made of hard-packed sand deposited by the river at some former period. A few inches below the top was a row of swallows' nests, close together, excavated in the bank. Every morning there was a great flight of swallows, setting forth for food, and in the evening they returned and sat in the doorways of the nests, with a tremendous chattering. When the river was high it would undermine the bank, and much sand would be caved down to maintain the wide bar of clean white sand, which at other times stretched from the foot of the bank to the water, where a line of barges was always loading with sand for the glass-works up and down the river.

Except at low water there was much traffic on the river: small passenger boats that made short trips up and down the river, and great side-wheel three-decker packets, which plied the river to Pittsburgh, Louisville, St. Louis, Memphis, and down to New Orleans. All of us boys knew by the sound of its whistle which of the big boats was coming 'round the bend from the east or west. Then there were the stern-wheel tow boats, handling great fleets of barges loaded with all sorts of commodities, coal from Pittsburgh predominating. At low water the stream was only a few feet wide, and could be waded, but when the annual freshets from melting snow swept down the stream it was a mighty torrent, sometimes ninety feet deep and two or three miles wide, dark brown with silt and carrying all kinds of flotsam, from mice to houses.

In normal times fishermen seined the river and sometimes caught a fish that I have never seen nor heard of elsewhere, called a Spoonbill, which had a bill like a duck's, but much larger. Sometimes they caught huge sturgeon, which caused them much grief, breaking the net and liberating the other fish. The sturgeon was not considered fit to eat, so they threw them back into the river. Many of the men in Dayton worked over in the city, and rowed across the river in skiffs. There were also skiff ferries and steam ferries, the fare being five cents. The great Roebling suspension bridge was built about this time, but it was at Newport, several miles down the river. I think it is still serving satisfactorily, with a greatly increased traffic.[7] The principal industry in Dayton was making hemp twine by hand in a number of little ropewalks.

When the war was over my father was put in charge of the Newsboys' Home, a municipal institution in Cincinnati, which was later merged with the Union Bethel, which overlooked the Public Landing on the river, the busiest place in town.[8] The Bostona, a big steamer which made daily trips up the river, tied up just below the Bethel, and early every morning her calliope played a popular tune, the words to which are, "Mother dear may I go swim, yes my darling daughter, hang your clothes on a hickory limb, and don't go near the water."

When I was five years old we moved to the Indian Territory, where my father was to superintend the activities of a new manual training school at Tullahassee in the Creek Nation, maintained jointly by the Presbyterian Home Mission Board and the Creek Indian Council.[9] We went on the "Fort Gibson," a new steamer built to ply between Cincinnati and Fort Gibson in the Indian Territory. This was a wonderful voyage, lasting three weeks, of which my most vivid recollection is that I had two hats blown away into the river, for which I got spanked, and that a squirrel in the park in Memphis, where we tied up a little while, clambered over me looking for something to eat in my pockets. From the Mississippi we went up the White River in Arkansas a few miles, then through a short canal to the Arkansas River, the mouth of which was blocked by sand bars, up the Arkansas to the Verdigris River, a few miles up the Verdigris, and then our part of the cargo was discharged in the woods and hauled to Tullahassee by ox teams.

The mission building stood alone in the woods, except for its outbuildings. It was of red brick, a hundred feet by fifty feet,

American Transformations

with an ell in the middle of one side, forty by sixty feet, and three stories high. There were about a hundred pupils, Creek boys and girls in their teens. Being under the auspices of a missionary society, with an ordained minister in charge, I suppose the chief aim was to inculcate the Protestant Christian religion, and secondarily to teach English, the three R's and certain kinds of manual labor, principally farming.[10] There was a large farm, a grist mill, a sawmill, and a shingle mill run by a steam engine. The field hands and the servants were all Negroes. It was said that there were more Negroes than Indians in the Territory. Before the Civil War many Indians had slaves. Our nearest neighbor, Colonel McIntosh, a Creek Indian, was said to have had a hundred slaves.[11]

This was a lovely fertile region of rolling prairie, interspersed with clumps and groves and forests of trees, a mild climate, a thick black soil and many watercourses, a truly rich country. The prairie grass was taller than I when we went there, with millions of prairie chickens, beautiful fowls, fine to eat. Once, the day before Thanksgiving, my father took his gun and a rope out onto the prairie in the early morning, and returned before noon with enough birds knotted into that rope on his back to furnish us all with fowl for Thanksgiving dinner. There were many turkeys also in the woods, and he shot enough of them for Christmas dinner. There were panthers in the woods, and sometimes I heard them screaming at night, a bloodcurdling sound.

There were four of us white boys, of which I was the youngest, and I had another playfellow of about my own age named Goliath, "Golly" for short. He was black as soot, the son of Aunt Rose, one of the cooks, a tall, lanky, solemn woman. His sole garment was a long white cotton shirt, like a night-shirt. Aunt Rose, who lived in a cabin nearby, owned some razor-backed hogs, and the big sows would stick their snouts under the rail fence, which enclosed the back yard and kitchen garden, and raise it up so their little pigs could get in, and follow them. I was supposed to drive them out whenever I saw them in the yard, but was strictly enjoined not to throw rocks at them. One day I threw a brickbat, and my aim was too good, for it killed a pig just as Aunt Rose came out of the kitchen door, and she raised an awful rumpus. Father paid her for the pig, I got a good switching, and we had roast pig for dinner.

The timber in the woods was mostly hardwood, oak, hickory, black walnut, and ash, but there were many big cottonwoods along the streams. My father, not aware of the propensity of cottonwood lumber to warp, sawed enough cottonwood lumber to fence the whole farm, and had a nice-looking fence; but in a little while his fence was gone, the boards having curled up, pulled out the nails, and fallen down. In the Arkansas River bottom he gut a giant black walnut tree, and from a single log, which it took twelve yoke of oxen to haul up to the mission, he sawed enough shingles to roof the whole building.

The main highway from Texas to Kansas City passed by our front yard, and immense herds of cattle sometimes came by.[12] This yard was a beautiful place, with a thick carpet of grass and many trees, hickory and black walnut and oak, one great walnut a few feet from the main front door, taller than the house, bearing ten barrels of nuts. Wild strawberries were plentiful in the woods, and not far away a great thicket of blackberries, where, when they were ripe, all of us went with a big wagon and picked blackberries until the wagon was heaped up with them. There were black haws and red haws and wild grapes in the woods, and pecans, but it was hard to get the pecans, for the crows ate them as fast as they got ripe.

Van's Lake, not far away, teemed with fish called Redhorse. The Indian fishermen would load a dugout canoe with big gourds, to each of which was attached a line with several baited hooks on it. Then they would distribute the gourds around the lake. Soon, a frantic bobbing and rushing around the gourds would ensue, and they gathered in the fish. A mile or two from the mission on the prairie was the outcrop of a coal seam, and they dug coal there for the steam boiler. My father raised sorghum, and got a cane mill and an evaporator to make syrup.

The motive power for the mill was a big black mule, hitched to the end of a long boom, while I sat on a board at the end of the boom and belabored him with a stalk of cane, while I chewed cane until my jaws ached.

The principal item on the bill of fare at the school was sofky, an Indian food. It was made of corn, pounded up in a hardwood mortar with a long heavy hickory pestle with a blunt point, wielded by two women, until it was about the size of hominy grits, when it was boiled until thoroughly cooked with enough water to make a rather thin gruel. The white folks usually ate their sofky fresh and hot, and we children were sometimes allowed a little sugar in ours, but the Indians preferred it sour, as they did milk and corn bread. I can't remember that we ever had white bread, but we had flour biscuits. Flour and sugar and coffee and tea and rice any many suchlike staples were more or less a luxury, and came from Cincinnati twice a year. Meat was plentiful, as we raised our own livestock, but butter was sometimes a little scarce, as there were hardly enough cows to furnish butter for so many. The Indians were very fond of butter, and used it lavishly when they could.

It was a fine country to live in, but it had its drawbacks. Venomous insects and snakes abounded. We boys used to get the little red scorpions and pit them against each other, and they would fight viciously until one killed the other. An adder bit one of the girls on the ankle and she died as a consequence.

My mother taught me to read and write and cipher while we lived there. After three years we went back to Dayton to live. My father gave up his job at the mission. We came by wagon to Baxter Springs, Kansas, thence by rail to Cincinnati. The Ohio & Mississippi Railroad from Cincinnati to St. Louis was of six-foot gauge, which made a lot of trouble and expense, so it was decided to change it to standard gauge.[13] As we came by on a Sunday, we could see men all along the line waiting for the train to pass, then prying up the rail on one side and shoving it over and spiking it down, so the gauge of the road was changed in one day.

My uncle, William Hasbrouck, who married my mother's sister, had a drug store on Baymiller Street in Cincinnati, and lived above the store, as most city storekeepers did.[14] My father thought that the schools in the city were better than those in Dayton, so early Monday mornings I took the horse-car over to Uncle William's and went to the Baymiller Street School. The principal of this big school was a little man named Scheidemantel, who had a pronounced German accent, and my first teacher was a Dresden shepherdess called Miss Vezey, also having a decided German accent. I adored her, with her pink cheeks and yellow hair and blue eyes, and was very anxious to please her, so I was a model pupil. My most intimate friend was a boy named Billy Procter, whose father, with a man named Gamble, had a soap factory in the middle of Baymiller Street on an oval piece of ground with a high board fence around it. The street, which was lined with stores on both sides, was divided to go around it. The factory was a collection of rough board shacks, and smelled to Heaven, and was a constant fire menace, but it stayed there a long time before they moved to the outskirts of the city and built their model plant at Ivorydale. Billy and I walked back and forth to school together, and when Uncle William saw me with him, he said, "I don't want you to go with that Procter boy. He's a bad boy." This of course made me only the more friendly with him.[15]

About the first recess at the school a lot of boys formed a ring with joined hands around me and danced about me and stuck out their tongues and pointed their fingers at me and shouted "N——, N——, N——." I was very indignant. I did not realize, in the three years of very young childhood association with Negroes, that I had acquired all their forms of speech. Of course I soon outgrew that "Southern drawl."

That Fall the great Chicago fire occurred, and we talked of it with bated breath while it was burning.[16] Cincinnati sent a train-load of men and apparatuses to help fight it. The first practical steam fire engine had been invented in Cincinnati by a friend of my mother's named Latta, and the city fire department had been equipped with them, and proclaimed itself the most efficient in the world.[17] It was the time of the hazy Indian Summer, when smoke from countless burning leaves filled the air, and it seemed to me that the smoke from the great fire was hovering over the whole country, and I was oppressed by the fear that such a calamity might visit us.

The part of the city where our school was located was called "Over the Rhine," because it was above the big canal which ran through the city, and was populated principally by Germans. In the evenings along Baymiller Street they would be sitting on the doorsteps and smoking their long-stemmed porcelain pipes. On Fridays I took the horse-car back to Dayton for the weekend at home.

When I was nine years old we moved to Greensburg, Indiana, a town of about five thousand people sixty-nine miles northwest of Cincinnati and forty-four miles southeast of Indianapolis, where my father bought a house and opened a music store.[18] There I was put in the fourth grade in school and my teacher was a big, good-natured, smart old maid, who spanked her offending pupils on her knee with a shingle, and made them get their lessons. This town was a beautiful place of well-built and well-kept houses, covering a gently rising knoll which was said to be the highest point in the state, and so was visible from all directions from afar. It was so embowered in trees that no houses were visible in summer, only the tall square tower of the court house standing above the trees, with a silver poplar tree at its top, growing out of the interstices between the stones of its roof, and with its quivering leaves glistening in the sun. I am told that this tree is still alive and vigorous.[19] It was a quiet well-to-do community, made up mostly of New Englanders and their descendants, with few foreigners.[20] Living was cheap and good, and wages and salaries correspondingly low. The highest paid man in town was the cashier of the First National Bank, who received $1,200 a year and owned a big fine house with a beautiful yard. There were few very rich people, but many with a competence and few in want.

My father was organist and choir leader for the Presbyterian Church. He tried to teach me to play the piano, but soon found that I had no talent for it and would be wasting my time trying to learn to play. I had a good voice and a natural aptitude for singing, so he taught me to sing, and bought songs for me to sing. He organized an amateur brass band and taught them and played the leading cornet. After a time the snare drummer left, and there was no other snare drummer in town, so my father taught me to play the little drum, and put me in the band. I was only thirteen, and when I donned my gorgeous uniform with red and gold braids and immense epaulettes and paraded with the band, I almost burst with pride. We had a good amount of playing to do, especially at election time. We sometimes played at the neighboring county fairs as well as at our own, and we sometimes gave concerts, and once a minstrel show.

When I was fourteen, my father took me out of school and put me to work for a year in a drug store. There I had to be on hand in the morning at six o'clock, and sweep the floor and sidewalk, build the fire in winter, dust, and do all the errands, help wait on customers, and do the many other things a cub in a drug store must do, until eight o'clock at night and until ten o'clock on Saturdays. In the intervals I had to study the United States Dispensatory, a huge volume like the International Dictionary, known as the "Druggist's Bible," as I was supposed to be learning the drug business. The proprietor was a graduate of the Philadelphia College of Pharmacy, the only school of the kind in the U.S. then, and also had a diploma as an M.D., a capable and conscientious druggist.[21] We made many of the things we sold: tinctures and extracts, pills and powders. We had a soda fountain, a rarity then, and made everything for it: gas for the water, syrups, and flavoring extracts. Every spring we got a wagonload of strawberries for strawberry syrup, and later a wagonload of blackberries for flavoring and wine and cordial. In the fall we got several barrels of cider to bottle and make vinegar from. So you see I had plenty to keep me occupied. After I started to school again I worked in the store in the mornings and evenings, before and after school.

In the high school we organized a debating society, which met once a week in the office of the sheriff in the courthouse in the evening. I took a leading part as a debater, and made up my mind to be a lawyer, but my father disapproved of that, having a poor opinion of the legal profession. Uncle William offered to bear the expense of my college course, if I would study to be a doctor, but I did not think I would make a good doctor, so I declined. I graduated from the high school in 1881 and still have my diploma, engrossed on real parchment.

I went to work at once on full time in the drug store, at a salary of fifteen dollars a month. By this time I was a prescription clerk, and put up many of the prescriptions.

About a year before this my father had secured a position as choirmaster in the Presbyterian church in Leadville, Colorado, a booming mining town, and had gone there. Soon after I got through school he sent for us to come there. I was enjoying life in Greensburg, and did not want to leave there, but my mother was sure that I would go to the dogs if she left me there alone, so she insisted that I go along.

Notes

1. Worcester's original typescript describes the author as "an ordinary native American," a phrasing that might confuse contemporary readers. Rightly, he never claimed indigenous heritage, and used the adjective "native" to claim an American-born ancestry generations deep.

2. Leonard Worcester's father, Leonard Sr., was born to Rev. Samuel A. Worcester and Ann (Orr) Worcester at Union Mission, Cherokee Nation, on March 8, 1836. Worcester Family Bible, Anne Worcester Coleman Rowe Papers (privately held), Dallas, Texas. Samuel Worcester proselytized among the Cherokee on behalf of the American Board of Commissioners for Foreign Missions, a Congregational organization. He cofounded with Elias Boudinot the *Cherokee Phoenix*, the first Native American newspaper, and is especially important historically for his work on behalf of the Cherokee to resist removal. This culminated in the Supreme Court case *Samuel A. Worcester v. The State of Georgia*, 31 U.S. (6 Pet.) 515 (1832), decided in favor of the Cherokee and Worcester but ignored by President Andrew Jackson, who forced the nation's removal on the infamous "Trail of Tears" to present-day Oklahoma. On missions, the Cherokee, removal, and Jacksonian America and beyond, see esp. Ronald A. Berutti, "The Cherokee Cases: The Fight to Save the Supreme Court and the Cherokee Indians,"

American Indian Law Review 17, no. 1 (1992); Grant Foreman, *Indian Removal: The Emigration of the Five Civilized Tribes of Indians* (Norman: University of Oklahoma Press, 1974 [1932]); Tim Alan Garrison, *The Legal Ideology of Removal: The Southern Judiciary and the Sovereignty of Native American Nations* (Athens: University of Georgia Press, 2009); Tiya Miles, *Ties that Bind: The Story of an Afro-Cherokee Family in Slavery and Freedom* (Berkeley: University of California Press, 2005); William G. McLoughlin, *Cherokees and Missionaries, 1789–1839* (New Haven: Yale University Press, 1984); Jill Norgren, *The Cherokee Cases: Two Landmark Federal Decisions in the Fight for Sovereignty* (Norman: University of Oklahoma Press, 2004); Theda Perdue and Michael D. Green, *The Cherokee Nation and the Trail of Tears* (New York: Viking, 2007); Theda Perdue and Michael D. Green, eds., *Cherokee Removal: A Brief History with Documents* (Boston: Bedford/St. Martin's, 1995); Julie L. Reed, *Serving the Nation: Cherokee Sovereignty and Social Welfare, 1800–1907* (Norman: University of Oklahoma Press, 2016); and Fay A. Yarbrough, *Race and the Cherokee Nation: Sovereignty in the Nineteenth Century* (Philadelphia: University of Pennsylvania Press, 2008).

3. Worcester attended St. Johnsbury Academy, established in 1842 by three brothers: Joseph, Thaddeus, and Erastus Fairbanks. The latter two developed and sold mechanical scales used to weigh agricultural produce. See esp. Fairbanks Family Papers (MSC 134–40), Vermont Historical Society Library (Barre, Vermont).

4. Dayton (Kentucky) is now part of the greater Cincinnati metropolitan area, on the south shores of the Ohio River.

5. Western Female Seminary, founded in 1853, became part of Miami University in 1974. Worcester's mother, Mary Roche Spooner, graduated from WFS in 1858. He mentions Carolyn (Scott) Harrison as a classmate, but she graduated from the Oxford Female Institute, a separate college for women in Oxford, in 1853. *Memorial: Twenty-Fifth Anniversary of the Western Female Seminary, Oxford, Ohio, 1880* (Indianapolis: Carlon & Hollenbeck, 1881), 61, 176.

6. Worcester confuses tribe with geography here. Spooner, with her sister, Lucy, served as a missionary and teacher in a boarding school among the Dakota for two years, based in Lac qui Parle, on the western edge of Minnesota Territory. Stephen R. Riggs, *Tah-Koo Wah-Kan; or, The Gospel among the Dakotas* (Boston: Cong. Sabbath-School and Publishing Society, 1869), 402–3; Stephen R. Riggs, *Mary and I: Forty Years with the Sioux* (Boston: Congregational Sunday School and Publishing Society, 1887), 147. See also the Stephen R. Riggs and Family Papers, Minnesota Historical Society (St. Paul, Minn.).

7. Indeed, the John A. Roebling Suspension Bridge predated his Brooklyn Bridge by seventeen years, and it survives to this day as a major thoroughfare between southwestern Ohio and northern Kentucky. See esp. Harry R. Stevens, *The Ohio Bridge* (Cincinnati: Ruter, 1939) and D. B. Steinman, *The Builders of the Bridge: The Story of John Roebling and His Son* (New York: Harcourt, Brace, 1945).

8. The Newsboys' Home was "intended for homeless newsboys and bootblacks," or shoe-polishers, "and most of the boys of this class avail themselves of its advantages. Meals are furnished to all newsboys and bootblacks at ten cents each, while the boys of the Home have the privileges of the bath-rooms, and are not charged for their lodgings." Cincinnati Union Bethel began as a way "to provide for the spiritual and temporal welfare of river men and their families." D. J. Kenny, *Illustrated Cincinnati: A Pictorial Hand-Book of the Queen City* (Cincinnati: Robert Clarke, 1875), 54, 56.

9. The Worcester family arrived in Tullahassee in October 1868, when Leonard Jr. was four years old. As superintendent, Leonard Sr. managed the business activities of the school, which had eighty students, funded in part by the Muscogee/Creek Council. *The Thirty-second Annual Report of the Board of Foreign Missions of the Presbyterian Church in the United States of America* (New York: Mission House, 1869), 9–10.

10. At the school, "the boys are taught to do the ordinary work of the farm, and the girls to sew and do general work." Leonard Worcester (Sr.) to Major F. S. Lyon, No. 112, *Report of the Commissioner of Indian Affairs to the Secretary of the Interior* (Washington: Government Printing Office, 1872), 578.

11. Worcester refers to Daniel N. McIntosh.

12. The Shawnee Trail was one of several routes that delivered cattle from southern Texas and the Mexican north to markets in the Midwest and East. For an excellent recent study of the market and environmental connections between these trails and the post–Civil War United States, see James E. Sherow, *The Chisholm Trail: Joseph McCoy's Great Gamble* (Norman: University of Oklahoma Press, 2018).

13. The Ohio & Mississippi Railroad changed its gauge in 1871. Douglas J. Puffert, *Tracks across Continents, Paths through History: The Economic Dynamics of Standardization in Railway Gauge* (Chicago: University of Chicago Press, 2009), 138.

14. Worcester's "mother's sister" here is Amanda J. Spooner, Mary's elder by nine years, and not their other sister, Lucy, who had accompanied Mary to the Dakota reservation in Minnesota Territory. William L. Hasbrouck was a prominent druggist, whose shop was located at York and Baymiller Street in Cincinnati.

15. Worcester mistakenly spelled his friend's surname as "Proctor," but census records confirm William C. Procter, son of William A. Procter, would have been around his age, though no evidence can be found to certify they were boyhood friends. The company he describes here, of course, was Procter & Gamble.

16. The Great Chicago Fire devastated the metropolis in 1871.

17. Alexander Latta developed the first steam fire engine in 1852.

18. The Worcesters moved to Indiana along with the Hasbroucks, who opened a pharmacy in Greensburg. After Lucy was widowed in 1873, she joined the extended family there as well.

19. Greensburg is still known for trees growing atop its courthouse, though the specific one changes over the years.

20. Worcester writes from the perspective of a settler-colonist, of course, defining "foreigner" as one not born in the United States. It is important to recall that all non–Native American residents were foreigners inhabiting lands around Greensburg once claimed by the Lenape/Delaware, Myaamia/Miami, and Shawnee Indians, among others.

21. By the 1870s the American Pharmaceutical Association had been established for twenty years. The professionalization and standardization of medical care still remained in its infancy. See "Code of Ethics of the American Pharmaceutical Association, Adopted in 1852," *Annals of the American Academy of Political and Social Science* 101 (May 1922), 267–68.

2

A Pragmatic Professional, 1881–1893

WE ARRIVED IN LEADVILLE ON AUGUST 10, AFTER A VERY hot journey. It had been raining there for five days, and the streets were a quagmire, and that night there was a heavy frost. I thought I had come to the jumping-off place sure enough, and I was homesick for Greensburg. Leadville is ten thousand feet above sea level, so winter comes early and stays a long time. Usually snow begins to fall early in October, and the ground does not appear again until May, so everything goes on runners for seven months or more.[1] The summers are very cool, and I have even seen flurries of snow on July Fourth, while the foot races were being run on the main street. No vegetables nor fruit can be grown there, so living is high.

The tales of the boom days at Leadville would fill many volumes. It was a "wide open" town. The doors of the gambling houses along the main street were never closed. Saloons, variety shows, and dance halls abounded and were liberally patronized. Shootings were frequent, and it was said there was "a man for breakfast every morning."[2] Not a very good place for a boy of eighteen after quiet, orderly Greensburg, where a man who frequented a saloon was not considered respectable and gambling was unheard of.

My father had acquired a controlling interest in a music store, and put me to work there. The first night after our arrival he took me with him to the meeting of the Apollo Club, the local singing society, of which he was the president, and introduced me into the club. Among the crowd of adventurers who came to Leadville were many well-educated and cultured people, so I had the privilege of association with a cosmopolitan community such as I could never have met anywhere else. Among them were some good singers, who joined the Apollo Club, which endured for more than twenty years. I went to Leadville for the twentieth anniversary of the club, and there were letters from former members all over the world. One of the members of the club was Asa Hutchinson, who for a long time had been the head of the "Hutchinson Family," a traveling group of singers who had sung in Greensburg two or three times while I lived there. There were many professional musicians there, playing in the variety shows and dance halls, and most of them made their "hangout" at father's store.[3]

He taught me to tune pianos and organs, and after a time I did most of that work, of which there was a good deal. But I did not like the store, and objected so much to working there that my father got me a job at the stamp mill owned by H. A. W. Tabor.[4] It was feeding a rock crusher, and I discovered from a remark that the superintendent let drop that my father and he had agreed to put me at a job so tough that I would soon tire of that kind of work, and be glad to go back to the store. So I stubbornly stayed with the job, although for a while I was terribly sore from the unusual exertion, and my hands were badly blistered from handling the shovel, but this soon wore off, and I got as hard as nails. I could handle a long-handled shovel as well as anybody.

In that mill the ore was first thoroughly dried. The crushing and pulverizing made a thick cloud of dust in the mill, which permeated my skin so that I was red as an Indian from top to toe. The ore was roasted with salt to chloridize the silver, and my working clothes were so saturated with chlorine that I could be smelled a long way off. When I went home my mother made me come in the back way and take off all my clothes in the wood-shed. (I suppose that chlorine also prevented us from having the smallpox, of which there was an epidemic while I worked at the mill. Many people died in the vicinity of the mill through which we had to pass to and from work, but none of the men who worked in the mill had the smallpox.) After the ore was roasted it was agitated with mercury in amalgamating pans, and the resulting gold-silver amalgam was heated in a retort to drive off the mercury, and the silver and gold molded into bars. After a few months the mill burned down, and I went to work for an English mining engineer, a friend of my father, to learn the mining engineering profession.

The Apollo Club had an orchestra as an auxiliary, and I learned to play the slide trombone enough to play in this orchestra. Later my father had me play it in a quartet of instruments in his choir, with the organ, I playing the tenor part. He had an old ballad horn at the store, a species of French horn with a mellower tone and a range better adapted to the tenor part than the trombone. He had me learn to play the ballad horn, which is played with the left hand, and the right had shoved into the bell to modify the tone and muffle it.

One night at choir rehearsal there was no tenor singer, so Father said, "Well, Len, you will have to sing tenor." But I said, "But I can't do it, I have never sung tenor." He said, "Yes you can. None of this church music is too high for you." So I sang tenor from that time on. I sang the part of Bunthorne in Gilbert and Sullivan's *Patience* in an amateur performance, and leading parts in many such things, and solos at concerts, so that, what with the choir singing and club singing, I sang a good deal.[5] That was the time of the heyday of the big minstrel shows, when they had a lot of fine ballad singers. I wanted to be a minstrel, but my father and mother threw up their hands at such a thought and declared that it was out of the question for a respectable person to be a minstrel singer, so I did nothing about it.

I had a chum whose father kept a store next to my father's.[6] The father made $75,000 on a lease on the Robert E. Lee Mine, so he sent the boy to New York to learn French and music and manners. He came back with enough French to order a meal from a French menu, and, being a musical prodigy, he played the piano without effort, but could not read music. He would attend a musical performance and afterwards play all the music on the piano from memory. He knew all the light operas and musical comedies popular at that time.

He wrote and composed the music for a musical comedy, which he called the "Blue Ribbon."[7] He had a musician write the piano score as he played it to him, and write the parts for the singers and the orchestra from that score. Then he organized a company of amateurs, of which I was one, to produce it in the Opera House. It seemed a very good musical comedy to me, and perhaps it was, but the performance must have been something terrible. There was no one connected with it who had the least training in such matters. I was the stage manager and had charge of the rehearsals and played a leading part. The composer played the piano at rehearsals and also played a prominent part in the performance. We had many friends, so we had a good audience and the composer got enough out of it to more than pay expenses. As for the company, all they wanted out of it was the fun of it. This boy wrote two more of these musical comedies, which the Blue Ribbon Comedy Company, as we called ourselves, gave in the Opera House to good audiences. Afterward the father bought a hotel in Omaha, and they went there, and I heard that the son drank himself to death, a sad ending to a promising career.

My first trip underground, a few days after I arrived in Leadville, was down into the A.Y. Mine, a quarter-interest which belonged to two Philadelphians, a Quaker and a Jew, who were said to have paid $30,000 each for their interests to the original locator. The mining engineer for whom I later worked was the consulting engineer for this mine, and Graham and Guggenheim came into his office on their visits from Philadelphia to talk with him and look over the maps.[8] They were an odd-looking pair, Graham a tall dignified man in a broadcloth Prince Albert coat with a low-cut vest and broad expanse of stiffly starched white shirt bosom and silk hat; Guggenheim a little man scarcely reaching to Graham's shoulder, with flat feet, baggy trousers, sack coat and derby hat. They seemed to be on the best of terms. Looking over a map on the high drawing-board, Graham would put his arm around Guggenheim's shoulder and would say, "Now you see it's like this, Guggy." Guggenheim afterward bought the other interests in the mine and the Minnie claim adjoining it, and sent one of his sons, Benjamin, to keep the accounts and look after the ore shipments. The foreman at the mine was a red-headed Nova Scotian named Sam Nicholson, who afterward made a large fortune in Leadville mining on his own account, and got elected to the United States Senate from Colorado.[9] I see by the last *Mining Journal* that his heirs and beneficiaries are stated to have agreed to pay the sum of $10,000 to the Colorado Mineral Resources Board for the purpose of beginning, planning, and making a complete survey of the proposed Leadville drainage tunnel, which it is hoped will give the old camp a new lease of life.

In 1886, the G.A.R. offered to hire me to take charge of their Juvenile Drum Corps, and get them in shape to go to San Francisco for the National Encampment that summer.[10] I agreed to do so, if they would put me in full control, so that I could expel any boy I wished to, or take in any boy I wished to, and their parents would consent that I might beat them with a drumstick as much as I chose. They agreed and the parents consented, and they were in pretty good shape by the time they were to go to San Francisco. The committee, which was to have raised the funds for the trip, failed to do so, and the boys were bitterly disappointed. They said that if I would make up some subscription lists and go out with them, they would try to get the money themselves. We needed $1,200. I made the lists, and in a few hours we had the money, so we set forth on schedule time. The boys had the time of their lives. They were all broke by the time we got to Ogden, but I doled out spending money during the rest of the trip.

When we stopped at the pier at Oakland to take the ferry for San Francisco, the Chief of Police of Oakland and his son, who was the captain of the Oakland Drum Corps, introduced themselves and said that they understood that our man in San Francisco had not been able to secure desirable lodgings for us. They had found some very good ones for us in Oakland, which they had engaged and paid for, and we were to be their guests. Also we were to eat free of charge whenever we wished at a big eating house, which the women's auxiliary had opened and would maintain during our stay.

We went with them and found that the lodgings were a new hotel, just finished and furnished, but not yet opened to the public. We were the only guests, and what a gang to inaugurate a brand new hotel. I spent much of my time the next few days trying to placate the proprietor for such things as overrunning a bathtub and spoiling a fine decorated ceiling, setting fire to a big velvet curtain while lighting a cigarette, and others ad infinitum. I think I have never seen such hospitality anywhere else as was shown these boys there. Someone was always doing something for them to give them a good time. They decided to have a parade of their own in Oakland a week after the parade in San Francisco, and asked us to stay for it, but I did not have money enough, so they gave me fifty dollars to cover the extra expense. Going home, when we got to Salida, Colorado, where we had to wait a few hours and change trains and eat a meal for which I had not planned, I was short of funds to pay for it. One of the boys had a counterfeit half dollar, which I passed on to the restaurant keeper, leaving us with 25 cents among us when we arrived home.

About this time a friend who had been living in Oakland, a fine bass singer, came home to visit his parents, and stayed through the winter and joined the Blue Ribbon Comedy Company. He urged me to go with him to Oakland in the spring, and said, if I would go, he would pay my way and my expenses until I got a job, and that if I did not want to stay, he would pay my way back. I had gone to work in my father's store some time before, as he said he needed me. He was loath to let me go, but he finally consented and gave me a hundred dollars for my expenses. We stopped three days in Salt Lake City, where we spent most of the waking hours in company with two Mormon girls, granddaughters of Brigham Young, and enjoyed ourselves hugely.

In Oakland the people with whom Harry had lived insisted that he should come and live with them again, and bring me with him. They treated him like a son. They lived in a big house on a corner, and on the other three corners of the street intersection were a synagogue, a Methodist church, and a Baptist church. We had a big room on a front corner upstairs, for which we paid sixteen dollars a month. Harry said, "The fleas will bother you a lot for a while, but you will get used to them. They won't bother me, for I got used to them when I lived here before." The fleas nearly ate him up, so that he hardly slept at all the first two or three weeks, but I slept peacefully. I am immune to most insect pests. There was one other roomer in the house, "Papa" Snow, the president of a bank, a handsome white-haired gentleman, who sang in the Congregational choir across the way, and was very friendly with us.

Our landlord was manager of the piano and organ department of the Bancroft Company, a big concern in San Francisco, and he was also the choirmaster of that big Congregational church, which was reputed to have the best choir on the Pacific Coast.[11] It consisted of thirty-two singers (all volunteers except a quartet of paid soloists), four on each of the eight parts to make a male and female chorus of sixteen each. There was a pipe organ and an amateur orchestra. He was able to maintain the choir on the basis that there was always a waiting list of applicants to join the choir, so he picked them only after careful examination as to their fitness. He at once restored Harry to his former position as bass soloist, and on his recommendation took me into the baritone section, where a vacancy occurred.

He had about fifty pianos of his own which he rented out in Oakland, Berkeley, and Alameda, and when he found out I was a piano tuner, he set me to getting his pianos in good condition while I looked for a job. Then he said that, if I could play the piano enough to show pianos to customers when no salesman was about, he would make me the house tuner at the Bancroft Company, the best job of the kind in San Francisco. I could not avail myself of his offer, as I could not play the piano. He said to look around, but not to take anything until I talked to him about it.

The next day I saw an ad for a stationery man, and answered it. I had some knowledge of the business, as shortly after I went to Leadville my father bought out a stationery store which occupied one side of the store room, of which his music store occupied the other side, and had continued to carry on the stationery business. The employment agency gave me a letter to Mr. Bancroft, who wanted a clerk in their stationery department. My landlord went with me and introduced me to Mr. Bancroft, and said, "If he accepts any job that you offer him, I guarantee that he will hold it down." He gave me a job at thirty dollars per month, but asked me not to tell the other clerks how much I was getting, as they had all started at twenty dollars per month.

Wages and salaries were much lower in San Francisco than those to which I had been accustomed in Leadville, except in the trades, which were fully union controlled. Harry was an iron molder, in good standing in the union, so he got a job at the Fulton Iron Works at once, at three dollars a day. Karl Formes, a famous German operatic bass, was teaching singing in San Francisco then, and Harry started studying under him right away, with a view to becoming a professional singer, which he did after a time.[12] The cost of living was in proportion to wages and salaries. I had breakfast and dinner at the best restaurant in Oakland, and lunch at a big "coffee house" in San Francisco, all of which cost me forty-five cents a day.

I enjoyed life there, but I kept getting indirect information that my father needed me very much. When the G.A.R. wired me an offer of $150 and my expenses from San Francisco to come and go with the Drum Corps to the National Encampment at St. Louis, I went back to Leadville and went to work in the store again. Mr. Bancroft said he was displeased at my

A Pragmatic Professional

going. He had expected me to stay on the job, and he was about ready to raise my wages to forty dollars a month and would do so, if I would stay. But I said that I thought it was my duty to go. He said that if I came back any time within the next two years, there would be a place for me.

The "Educational Department," in which I was employed, in addition to books and stationery, carried all kinds of school furniture and supplies, including a line of text books for all grades up to high school, which they published in their own printing house. The department did an average business of about $400 a day, and the manager, who had worked for them eleven years, and who Mr. Bancroft said was the best man in his line on the Coast, had a salary of seventy-five dollars a month. When Mr. Bancroft offered me my job in the first place, he said, "Thirty dollars a month may seem a small salary to you, but we pay the smallest salaries in San Francisco, because anyone who works for us can get a job somewhere else at a higher salary. We have the pick of the young men of San Francisco." I found this to be true, for shortly before I left, I was offered a job at seventy-five dollars a month by the largest retail book and stationery store in the city, solely because I held a job in that department at Bancroft's. The proprietor said, "You do not need any recommendations. If you can hold a job under Wilson, you can have mine." I declined that offer because I found that I would have to work from 7 a.m. to 9 p.m. every day in the week including Sunday, except Saturday, when I would work until 10 p.m.

I went to St. Louis with the Drum Corps. It was just the time of equinoctial storm, and it rained almost continuously the five days we were there. One of the members of the drum corps committee of the G.A.R. who went with us that trip was a real publicity agent. He found a reporter on one of the papers whose parents lived in Leadville, and he gave us a lot of publicity. He had hired a twelve-year-old boy, who was playing cornet solos at one of the variety shows, to go with us. We had Zouave uniforms that would attract attention a long way off, and an eight-year-old boy who looked like a cupid rode a burro in front and carried a gold-fringed white silk banner with our name in gold. The bass drum had an ornamental sign on one head. There were many drum corps there from all over the country, and they were a sorry lot, for with so much moisture in the air their drumheads were like dishrags. Our publicity man had us dry our drums in the hotel laundry, got closed carriages, and took us to the great Southern Hotel, where two of the most famous of the drum corps were quartered, with their drums stacked up in the lobby, sitting around disconsolately.

The Southern Hotel occupied a whole city block, with a rectangular court having a glass roof and a wide balcony all around on every floor, with a wide entrance in the middle of each side. There was a Turkish bath adjoining one of these entrances, with a door from the street and one into the wide entry that led to the central court. We slipped quietly out of our carriages into the hot room of the Turkish bath and dried our drums, quietly formed in the wide entry in open order, and, with a crash like the crack of doom in that confined space, down we went across the court to the opposite entrance, back to the center, at a right wheel to another entrance, back across the court to the opposite entrance, and finally formed a circle in the center of the court, playing all the time. We put our cornetist on the newel post of the big staircase, and he played Schubert's "Serenade."[13]

The fellows in the other drum corps were nonplussed, and tapped our drums and said, "How do you make them sound like that?" Their drums made no more noise than a blanket. We made no other explanation than that our drums were the very best made, and that we kept them properly overhauled. We put on some such a show at the other big hotels, where other drum corps were staying, and at the G.A.R. headquarters, and had all the other drum corps guessing.

The big parade was put off one day on account of the rain, but the next morning it was as bad as ever. I got some thin rubber cloth and tied it over the drumheads so that it just rested on them, with a stout string around the top hoop of the drums. We

A Pragmatic Professional

dried our drums in the laundry of the hotel and went in closed carriages to the point where we were to join the parade. The other drum corps were plodding by in the mud and rain, not making a sound, but we played all through the parade, and by "Uncle Billy" Sherman, who was in the reviewing stand, gave us a cheer as we passed, playing "Marching Through Georgia."[14]

We went to the annual National Encampments for several years after that, in Columbus, Detroit, Nashville, Washington, and Boston. Some of the boys who belonged to the corps became well known later. Matt Keefe, the famous yodeler, was a skinny little bell-hop in the Vendome Hotel at Leadville, who sang through his nose. One of the boys who joined when the corps was first organized, and succeeded me as leader, is president of a great international mining concern with offices on Fifth Avenue, New York.

With the output of the mines dwindling and the prices of silver and lead declining, I could see that the time must come when my father could no longer make the store pay a profit. When I got married in 1889, I went to Denver on my honeymoon and secured a job in the repair shop of the music company, which had sold the store in Leadville to my father.[15] I did not go to work at once, as I wanted a little vacation first. Some friends of mine, who operated a sampling works in Leadville and bought the ore from the A.Y. Mine, formed a company and built a fine smelter at Pueblo.[16] I was told that Meyer Guggenheim furnished most of the capital, and was represented in the company by his son, Ben, who had an office at the smelter as Secretary. One of the sampling-works' men was the president and general manager, and the other sampling-works' man was vice-president and treasurer.

My wife and I went to Pueblo to visit a couple who had both belonged to the Blue Ribbon Comedy Company. The husband was working at the new smelter, so I went out to see it and ran into the vice-president out in the ore yard. He said, "What are you doing here?" I said, in jest, "Looking for a job." He said, "You don't really mean that, do you? You don't need a job." I said, "Yes, I do." He said he did not have any job then that I would take, but he might have one any day, and if I would leave him my address, he would wire me. I gave him my address in Denver. I had had no idea of looking for a job there, but now I thought I might do much better if I could learn the smelting business than to plug along all my life as a piano repair man. I decided to take any job at the smelter that might be offered me.

The next day I got a wire to come and go to work. The job was bucking samples at the sampling mill of the smelter; preparing the ore samples for the assayer; and looking after the men who ran the ore-crushing rolls in the sampling mill and cut the samples down, and the men who took the moisture samples and dried them. There was plenty of work in this job, but it might lead to a job as foreman of the sampling mill or assistant to the assayer or chemist, the usual line of promotion in the smelting business. All went well, and I was hoping soon to have the better job that had been promised me, when one day the smelter seemed alive with Guggenheims, all of Meyer's sons having come visiting us.

Every now and then one or two of them would bring me samples to buck for them and say nothing about it. In a few days they had bought out the Leadville men and taken possession of the smelter, with Murry Guggenheim as president, entirely ignorant of the smelting business, but with a new general manager, who had built the successful Pueblo Smelting & Refining Company plant and had been its general manager. Immediately wages and salaries were cut and work increased, and many of the best men quit.

The superintendent told me that I must take the moisture samples, in addition to my other work, without any increase in wages. I said that would be impossible, as I should have to be in two places in the same time sometimes, and reminded him that he had promised me more pay and a better job soon, when I went to work there. He said that would be impossible at that time, so I went to the office and got my check. Ben Guggenheim saw me there and asked me why I was quitting. He said

A Pragmatic Professional

they were losing $2,000 a day, and must retrench, and advised me to stay and try handling both jobs at once. If I couldn't manage it, they would put the moisture man on again. I did not care to try it. I got a job as a supply clerk for an old friend from Leadville, a building contractor who was putting up a lot of buildings in Pueblo. Pretty soon his business fell off so that he did need me, and I did not see any prospect for a job in Pueblo, so I went back to Leadville.

I went to see the head of the drum corps committee of the G.A.R., who was manager of Senator Tabor's mines, and told him I wanted a job. "What kind of job do you want?" he said. I said, "I want to run a hoist." He said, "Did you ever run a hoist?" I said, "No, but I know how, and can do it." But he had no hoist that he could give me just then, and I had to go to work right away, so he gave me a job as trammer underground until he should have a hoist for me to run, which he promised would be soon. That job was a hard one for me. I was not very husky, and it was a job for a husky man, but I managed to hold it down until the hoist job was ready.

Most of the miners at that mine were Cornishmen, generally called "Cousin Jacks" among the mining fraternity. They were the best miners in the world, their forefathers having been miners for more than two thousand years but with a reputation for being averse to giving more than a minimum of service for their wages.

Sometimes, when I trundled the big ore bucket into the stope to fill it up, a voice would float down saying, "Trammer, do you know Red Mike?" If I said, "yes," sounds of activity continued above, but if I said "no," they ceased at once, and the voice would say, "Well, let's touch pipe." My answer indicated whether or not the foreman was in sight.

There were some queer hoists in Leadville in those days, and my first one was one of them. It was a one-cylinder steam engine, and the drum on which the cable was wound was manipulated by a single lever, which, shoved one way, pushed it against paper friction wheels to hoist, and, the opposite way, pushed it against a block of wood fastened to the frame for a brake. If any of the three connections between the hand and the drum should break, or the pin which held it should slip out, the drum would be free, and the cable would quickly unwind and go to the bottom of the shaft. The first thing I did was to shove a long stick of timber over the engine frame, with its end under the drum, so that I could bear down on it as an emergency brake. There was a heavy fly-wheel, so that I could start the loaded bucket from the bottom of the shaft without sticking on the center, if I gave the cable a little slack and opened the throttle quickly enough.

One day, when I was alone hoisting men, the key that held the wheel on the shaft slipped out, and the wheel came off and rolled over against the wall. I managed to roll it back to its place, and, with blocking and a pry, raised it the little distance necessary for me to push it back onto the shaft. After a while they installed a better hoist and a bigger boiler, and I worked there more than a year, when, having failed to find ore in paying quantity there, I was transferred to another shaft.

Hoist men in those days usually worked seven days in the week, and two hoist men would divide the twenty-four hours between them as they pleased, usually the day shift man working from 7 a.m. to 5 p.m., and the night shift man from 5 p.m. to 7 a.m., so as to give the day man a little more time to sleep in the morning and a little more time for recreation in the evening. We changed shifts every two weeks, working each nineteen hours to make the change. For this we received four dollars a day. The long night shift wasn't so bad, if I was kept busy, but when the trips were far apart I would fall asleep in the chair. The sound of the gong would bring me to my feet, grasping the levers with my eyes shut, so that I had to pry one open to see the mark on the cable or indicator.

At the new place they were sinking a big deep shaft with a big hoist, converted from a sawmill engine. I lost this job because I burned out a bearing on the hoist, but they put me on as a carpenter for a while, and then on the pumps, when they got down to where there was so much water they had to have a gang of pump men. After a while the water got the best of them, so I lost that job.

I got a job running a big stationary engine at a smelter, while the night-shift man went on a month's vacation. The shift was from 6 p.m. to 6 a.m., and as there was usually very little to keep me occupied, my chief job was keeping awake. I was alone, and read until I could no longer keep my eyes open, and smoked a lot. I had never played solitaire then, or I might have resorted to that to keep me awake. I did not dare to go to sleep, so I would pace up and down to keep awake.

Then I got a job at Kokomo, a mining camp about thirty-five miles from Leadville, another all-night-shift job, running an air compressor, firing an old leaky boiler with wood and sharpening the drills by hand for a pair of big drilling machines driving a tunnel in granite. That is a snowy country, and by Thanksgiving Day that year the snow lay seventeen feet deep on the flat below town. For two days it blew and snowed so that we could not get from one house to another in the little town. The man who had held the job before me came back after a little while and wanted the job back, and as he was a friend of the superintendent, I got let out.

About this time the great boom at Creede, in southwestern Colorado, got well started, and I thought I might have a chance to make some money there. I wrote the manager of one of the mines there who was my friend, who said they had no machinery, but he could put me on as a miner. Creede was a red-hot boom.[17] There was already a railroad there before the boom began, so it was easy to get to. There were two hundred men on the train I went in on, and the number increased daily until at the peak there were seven hundred a day. Some six hundred carpenters were busy night and day, building houses and stores and saloons, and when the train came into the station the sound of the hammers was like hail on a tin roof. On a sidetrack up the cañon there was string of Pullman cars two miles long, jam-full at regular Pullman rates.

Sometime before the boom, D. H. Moffatt, president of the First National Bank of Denver and of the Denver & Rio Grande Railroad, and the manager of his Maid of Erin Mine at Leadville, Eben Smith, had bought a mine near Creede called the "Holy Moses." The D.&R.G. Railroad had a branch line to Wagon Wheel Gap, eight miles from Creede, and it was soon after extended to Creede, presumably to furnish transportation for the Holy Moses ore. At the next stockholder's meeting Moffatt was deposed as president of the railroad, it was said, because of building that eight miles of road. When I went to Creede it was said that that eight miles of road was making more profit than all the rest of the D.&R.G. road. The line was so congested with freight for Creede that shippers often had to wait a long time, and all sort of things were shipped in by express, such as flour and sugar, mining tools, powder, fuse and caps, stoves, corrugated iron, nails, and I even saw two big anvils unloaded one day from an express car.

I arrived late in the afternoon, and was told that there would be no one going to the mine that day. The only place I could find to spread my bedroll was under a billiard table in a saloon on a sawdust-covered floor, for which the bartender charged me thirty-five cents. Just then someone said, "There goes a wagon for the Last Chance. If you run, maybe you can catch it." I grabbed my bedroll, and ran and yelled, and the driver stopped and took me aboard. I got to the mine before dark, and had a good supper and bed at the manager's house.

Creede was one of those fabulous discoveries of high-grade silver ore cropping out on the surface. A farmer and a butcher in Del Norte, a town in the nearby San Luis Valley, grubstaked a couple of prospectors, and they found about a wheelbarrow load of rich silver ore sticking out of a big vein. When they worked on it, it soon opened out into a great body of ore. One of the prospectors soon sold his interest for $10,000, and presently the other prospector and the butcher sold for $15,000 each, but the farmer held onto his interest, and it made him a rich man. They formed a company in Denver with a capital of $300,000, and put a lot of men to work. When I went there they were shipping seventy tons of ore a day, containing three hundred to five hundred ounces of silver per ton, all taken out by hand from two short tunnels, and by windlass from two fifty-foot shafts. The vein was sixteen feet wide, and all good ore, so it was shipped just as it came out, without any waste to be sorted out. Much of the ore was a beautiful amethyst quartz, in which no silver could be seen with the naked eye, but it was the best ore in the vein.

The claim next to the Last Chance on the vein was called the "Amethyst," and that was the name given to the new town, building down where the cañon was wider than at Creede, which was a one-street village in a narrow cañon with high vertical walls, so that the sun only shone an hour a day. The Amethyst Mine had its ore packed three miles down a steep icy trail to the railroad, on big Missouri mules that carried three hundred pounds to the load, but the Last Chance had a road, so their ore was hauled in wagons. The ore haulers there and at Leadville were the most expert teamsters I have ever seen. With big heavy wagons, piled high with ore, the loads averaging about five tons, they would go down those steep, crooked, rough roads, full of chuckholes, sometimes coated with ice or deep in mud or in a cloud of dust, almost on a run, with seldom a spill or serious mishap. At Leadville the horses were mostly big beautiful Clydesdales or Percherons, and cost a lot of money.

There were three big bunkhouses for the men, in the woods above the mine, near a big spring. They were known as the "Bull Pen," the "Boar's Nest," and the "Palace." The Bull Pen was like a logging camp bunkhouse, of logs, with a door at each end but no windows; a big square hole in the middle of the roof with a slab chimney built up from it, through which the stovepipe ascended to provide ventilation; two tiers of bunks of rough boards along each side, two men to each bunk, who furnished their own bedding and mattress, if they enjoyed such a luxury; and no floor but plank runways along the front of the bunks.

The men carried in their own water for drinking and washing from the spring, but a man from the cook-house brought in the wood. The Boar's Nest was a good, tight hewed-log building, with windows and a rough board floor and a ceiling, but the ventilation was very poor, the ceiling was pretty low, and the windows were not capable of being opened. The air was usually pretty thick. The Palace was newer than the other, built of rough lumber, with a floor, a high ceiling, big windows that could be opened, and single iron bedsteads.

I took up my residence in the "Bull Pen," as all other quarters were full. My bunkmate, in an upper bunk, was a young fellow who had been a hoistman in Leadville. We bought a straw mattress for our bunk, the only kind available in Creede then. As I preferred to work on the surface, the manager put me in charge of a gang building a new road to the mine.

It was January. The snow averaged about five feet deep and the ground was frozen deeper than that. We would drive a row of moil holes into the frozen ground above the bank on the upper side of the road we were building, along the hillsides, and shoot it down. I used to make the primers—sticks of dynamite with cap and fuse inserted—and range them, and the dynamite necessary for a round of holes, around a fire outdoors to warm them up before loading the holes. One day the dynamite caught fire from a spark, and burned up and I made no effort to rescue it, but stayed at a safe distance until it had burned up. A Swede working on the gang laughed at me and said, "Why don't you put out the fire?" I said, "I think it would be foolish for me to risk my life for a few sticks of powder." I had him go down to the powder house and make a new set of primers, and put the powder about the fire to warm. It caught fire and burned up, and he made no effort to put out the fire, so we were quits. I once saw a hoistman, when some dynamite in a cupboard in the hoisthouse had caught fire, shovel the burning powder from the cupboard and scatter it around the dump, as coolly and deliberately as if he were throwing out a shovel full of trash.

A Pragmatic Professional

The manager told me he had already ordered a hoist. He was going to sink a big deep shaft, and said for me to get a man that I was sure was all right, and when the hoist came for us to set it up and run it. That was the easiest hoist to handle that I have ever had my hands on, and almost noiseless. When the shaft was down about eighty feet, the snow suddenly began to melt, and a lot of water seeped down into that big loose vein, and I had to hoist as much as four hundred big buckets of water a shift. We had no pump nor valve bucket, so I had to use an ore bucket. With that hoist I could start a big bucket full of water from the bottom of the shaft so gently, and set it down on the platform at the top of the shaft so easily, that no water would be spilled. I made a siphon of two-inch pipe just big enough to empty one bucket while we hoisted another, so that by changing it quickly from one bucket to the other we could keep it going steadily, taking the water out the door, where it would run down the hill. I noticed that the manager was much interested in that siphon, and the next day he told me that he was going to siphon the water out of the mine. When he found out that he could not do it, he was sore at the other hoistman, who had told him that it could be done, and recommended that he do it.

The butcher who had sold his interest in the Last Chance Mine never ceased to lament it. When I went there he was running the boarding house, and he seemed to be trying to make the money out of the boarding house that he had failed to get for the mine, for the food was very poor. After a while we all made a complaint, and said we would not eat there any more, if there was not an improvement. So the manager got a famous boarding-house keeper from the Mary Murphy Mine at St. Elmo, a fine cook, and after that we had the best food I have ever eaten at a mine boarding house. We filled our own lunch buckets. After the meal, just before we went on shift, we filed through the kitchen between two long tables. Everything there was for lunch laid out in cafeteria style. Each man took his bucket from a rack as he came in, and selected what he wanted to eat and drink, and put it in, and then went on out the back door to work. There was always plenty of variety, good quality, well cooked.

Creede is in the foothills overlooking a wide fertile valley, where the farmers and ranchmen raise an abundance of almost everything to eat, including livestock, poultry, and dairy products. Food was fresh and cheap. The Amethyst Mine was the northernmost of the mines working on the great vein, but the vein was generally believed to extend for a long distance in that direction. The ground was covered deeply by glacial drift, and nobody had sunk a shaft deep enough to find out if the vein was there. The ground next to the Amethyst was owned by an old Irishman who worked at the Last Chance and two Swedes who lived in a cabin on the claim. Many of the hundreds of promoters, who thronged the camp looking for mines or prospects to capitalize, had tried to secure the ground by option or purchase, but without success, as the owners were all suspicious of one another, and could never agree on a price and terms.

One day my brother's father-in-law, a mining man from Black Hawk, came to see me. He said, "I have been here three weeks now, trying to find something for some Denver people, and I have combed the camp over and found only two places I want, and I can't get them. I believe that you could get them, and if you can get options that you can turn over to me, we will give you a ten percent commission, if we buy them." This was the opportunity that I had in mind when I went to Creede, so I got the Irishman, with whom I was friendly, to give me an option on his interest, provided I got one from each of the others on the same terms, the price to be $100,000 cash. Then I saw the Swedes separately, and told them what "Dad" Mahoney had agreed to, and got options from them, with the stipulation that I put ten men to driving a tunnel on the ground within twenty-four hours, and keep them there during the option. I hurried to town with the options, and my man wired Denver, and took the ten men up and put them to work driving the tunnel. He was much pleased, and said that they would surely buy that ground. They did not care whether it had anything on it or not, as on

A Pragmatic Professional

the strength of its location alone they could sell a million dollars' worth of stock. Then I had no difficulty in securing the other option he wanted, which was on a claim supposedly covering the other end of the big vein, at a price of $100,000. So it looked like I stood a good chance to clean up $20,000 in the next thirty days, and I was feeling pretty hopeful.

There was a huge man from Leadville who went by the name of "Big Foot Rube," whom I knew, looking around for something, for a Jew clothing man in Leadville. He heard a whispered rumor that the big vein turned at right angles about the middle of the "Amethyst" claim, and went out the sideline of the claim, instead of continuing on through the north endline. The Amethyst was strictly guarded, and none but employees were allowed underground. But the Last Chance had a drift connecting with the Amethyst workings, and Rube had free access to the Last Chance. So he got into the Amethyst with a compass and tape, and found the rumor to be true.

As soon as he came out he told some of us Leadville fellows what he found out, and then and there we formed a syndicate with ten shares, and sent down town for a surveyor. He came with snowshoes, measured along the line of the Amethyst to where Rube's measurement indicated that the vein crossed, and, following his course, ran out a line for two thousand feet to get beyond ground which we knew was held by a rich company, whose ground we did not dare to "jump" (although, they probably did not have valid title to it, having discovered no vein before making their location, as the law required). Here we shoveled away the snow, and started a shaft in the loose ground, which was more than twenty feet thick, searching for the vein. We were on ground held by the manager and bookkeeper of the Last Chance under location, so that night they sent men up with guns and drove us off, but we did not have to move far to get off their ground. When we got down to solid ground we came right down on top of a vein about two feet wide, and a sample from it assayed two ounces silver per ton, so under the law it was an ore-bearing vein, and we could make a valid location.

We got four well-known mining men to come and take a sample, then took them to all the shafts whose ground might conflict with our prospective locations, so they could certify that none of them had a vein at that time. We found that, when we had moved, we had landed on a wedge of ground seven hundred feet long, thirty feet wide at one end—tapering to a point at the other, which had been overlooked in the mad scramble for claims, which covered the hillside, overlapping one another like a bunch of jackstraws—and in one place seventeen [feet] deep. We located two claims, each fifteen hundred feet long by three hundred feet wide, with the endline between them at our shaft, extending across a lot of other claims. We sunk our shaft down 125 feet, but found no pay ore, so we stopped work.

After a while we sold our claims to the company that had the big group of claims between us and the Amethyst, with a deep shaft and a big plant but no valid title to its ground. They applied for a patent on the claims, and the first day after the application was filed there were seventeen adverse claims filed with which they conflicted; but they beat them all in court, and got the patent. They paid us what we had spent on the property, and gave us forty thousand shares of their stock. They found good ore, and the stock paid dividends for some years. Of course the news of the diversion of the big vein soon got abroad, and within twenty-four hours the Creede boom had burst.[18] The next day my man from Denver told me he had taken the men off the tunnel. He said, "There's no use going ahead with those options. You couldn't sell twenty-dollar gold pieces in Creede now for ten dollars." The camp settled down to the normal life of a lively mining camp.

About this time came "Soapy" Smith from Denver, with a gang of about forty thugs and gamblers, and took practical possession of the town.[19] I had seen him in Leadville, where he used to come peddling his soap. He would stand in the street just off the curb, with a small open suitcase hung in front of him by a strap around his neck. In the suitcase was a lot of little oblong pieces of white soap, a pile of slips of colored wrapping paper

A Pragmatic Professional

and a pile of paper money, from one-dollar to twenty-dollar bills. He would make a talk about the merits of his soap, meanwhile swiftly wrapping the little pieces of soap in the colored paper, and occasionally wrapping up a bill with one of them. When he had a sufficient group gathered and a pile of soap wrapped up, he would announce that he would sell this wonderful soap for only $1 a package, not making any mention of the money. Usually the money poured in as fast as he could make change and the soap was soon sold. Sometimes a buyer would actually get a twenty-dollar bill.

I saw that my chances for making quick money in Creede had vanished, and I would probably be better off in Leadville, so I went back and got a job on pumps again.

Notes

1. Leadville was at the peak of its rush when the Worcesters arrived in 1881, more than a year after the family patriarch, who appeared in the *Evening Chronicle* on June 10, 1880. On the early history of Leadville, see Don L. Griswold and Jean H. Griswold, *The Carbonate Camp Called Leadville* (Denver: University of Denver Press, 1951), and their *History of Leadville and Lake County, Colorado: From Mountain Solitude to Metropolis* (Denver: Colorado Historical Society, 1996), and Phyllis Dorset, *The New Eldorado* (New York: Macmillan, 1970).

2. This phrase was used by Mark Twain to describe California mining towns in his *Roughing It* (1872). Others like Daniel Pidgeon adopted it to describe both Leadville and Cheyenne, Colorado, in his *An Engineer's Holiday, or, Notes of a Round Trip from Long. 0° to 0°*, 2nd ed. (London: Kegan Paul, 1883), 108, 155. Charles Howard Shinn borrowed it to describe old timers of the Comstock Lode in his *The Mine II* (New York: Brampton Society, 1908), 246.

3. The arts scene in Leadville was notable and attracted major shows, including those by William F. "Buffalo Bill" Cody, and famous lecturers, as in the case of Oscar Wilde. See Gretchen Scanlon, *A History of Leadville Theater: Opera Houses, Variety Acts and Burlesque Shows* (Charleston SC: History Press, 2012), and Scott Gac, *Singing for Freedom: The Hutchinson Family Singers and the Nineteenth Century Culture of Antebellum Reform* (New Haven: Yale University Press, 2007). On the importance and centrality of music to central Colorado, see Henry Miles, *Orpheus in the Wilderness: A History of Music in Denver, 1860–1925* (Colorado Historical Society, 2006).

4. Horace Tabor was a mining magnate influential in Leadville cultural and political life, first as mayor and then as lieutenant governor of Colorado from 1879 to 1883. He served briefly in the United States Senate in 1883. See David Karsner, *Silver Dollar: The Story of the Tabors* (New York: Covici-Friede, 1932); Duane A. Smith, *Horace Tabor: His Life and the Legend* (Boulder: Colorado Associated University Press, 1973).

5. W. S. Gilbert and Arthur Sullivan, *Patience, or Bunthorne's Bride: A Comic Opera in Two Acts* (Boston: Ditson, 1881). See also Carolyn Williams, "Parody and Poetic Tradi-

tion: Gilbert and Sullivan's 'Patience,'" *Victorian Poetry* 46, no. 4 (Winter 2008), and John Bush Jones, ed., *W. S. Gilbert: A Century of Scholarship and Commentary* (New York: New York University Press, 1970).

6. Harry B. Iszard, Worcester's "chum," was the son of John and Anna Iszard and was three years younger than Worcester. Iszard's father was identified as a miner on the 1880 federal census, and Harry worked for the *Leadville Democrat-Herald* and as a miner while writing musicals and operas. The family later moved to Custer County, Nebraska, where Iszard wrote for the *Custer County Chief* as well as literary publications. *Corbell & Ballenger's Eighth Annual Leadville City Directory Containing a Complete List of the Inhabitants, Institutions, Incorporated Companies, Manufacturing Establishments, Business, Business Firms, etc. in the City of Leadville for 1887* (Leadville: Corbett & Ballenger, 1887), 154; *History of Custer County, Nebraska: A Narrative of the Past, with Special Emphasis upon the Pioneer Period of the County's History, Its Social, Commercial, Educational, Religious, and Civil Development from the Early Days to the Present Time* (Lincoln, Nebraska: Western Publishing & Engraving, 1919), 359.

7. The comedy company put on most of its plays in the latter 1880s, when Worcester and Iszard were in their early to mid-twenties, and it was through this company that Worcester first met another performer, and later his wife, Gertrude Beede. Of the Blue Ribbon Comedy Company's first titular performance, "A Blue Ribbon," a reviewer wrote that the "play was a decided amateur production in every sense, but it gave promise of better things, public confidence was inspired, and it became very evident that there was better amateur dramatic talent in the city than was popularly supposed. The next production by this company was 'A Silver Spoon,' and the performance and play was a revelation in amateur theatricals. The comedy—written by Mr. Iszard—was one of the cleverest and neatest things ever put upon the stage in our city, and the company that appeared in it were up to every requirement the little play needed. Taken all in all it was probably the best amateur performance ever given in the city, and the public was loud in praise of the commendable production." "The Amusement World," *Leadville Herald Democrat*, December 25, 1887, 4. See also "Very Successful Affair," *Leadville Herald Democrat*, September 6, 1887, 4; "Musical Melange," *Leadville Herald Democrat*, April 29, 1888, 3; "The Ribbon Company," *Leadville Herald Democrat*, April 30, 1888, 3.

8. Worcester is likely referring to the mining engineer David W. Brunton, who worked for Charles Graham and Meyer Guggenheim on the A.Y. Mine and others. "David W. Brunton: An Interview," in T. A. Rickard, *Interviews with Mining Engineers* (San Francisco: Mining and Scientific Press, 1922), 69–95. On the early history of the A.Y. Mine, focusing on Graham and Guggenheim, see "The Guggenheims and the Smelting Industry," *Mining and Scientific Press* 122, no. 6 (February 5, 1921), 179–82. Contemporaries attributed the Guggenheim fortune to their early investments in the A.Y. and Minnie Mines. "Started the Guggenheim's Vast Fortunes," *Lead and Zinc News* 8, no. 2 (June 27, 1904), 84; Stephen Birmingham, *"Our Crowd": The Great Jewish Families of New York* (Syracuse, New York: Syracuse University Press, 1996 [1967]), 225–29.

9. Samuel Nicholson served in the U.S. Senate from 1921 to 1923.

10. The Grand Army of the Republic, an organization of Union veterans, was formed after the Civil War and held "national encampments" annually, to which various local posts would send representatives and drum and bugle corps. Robert Burns Beath, *History of the Grand Army of the Republic* (New York: Willis McDonald, 1888); Stuart McConnell, *Glorious Contentment: The Grand Army of the Republic, 1865–1900* (Chapel Hill:

A Pragmatic Professional

University of North Carolina Press, 1992); Barbara A. Gannon, *The Won Cause: Black and White Comradeship in the Grand Army of the Republic* (Chapel Hill: University of North Carolina Press, 2011).

11. In 1871 the A. L. Bancroft Company opened a music department, managed by William Henry Knight, as an extension of its famed publishing company, first begun by Hubert Howe Bancroft in 1852. *Bancroft's Tourist's Guide. Yosemite. San Francisco and Around the Bay (South.)* (San Francisco: Bancroft, 1871), vii. After founding the company, Hubert focused on producing monumental works on the history of the American West, broadly conceived. Bancroft's interpretations have since yellowed with age, but his contribution to western historiography formed the early contours of the field.

12. Formes had a distinguished career and was, according to one obituary, "at one time the greatest basso profundo on the operatic stage." "Herr Karl Formes: Death of the Once Famous Basso of the Operatic Stage," *Daily Alta California* 81, no. 169 (December 16, 1889), 1. He died in San Francisco in 1889, and his autobiography was published posthumously. See Karl Formes, *My Memoirs. Autobiography of Karl Formes* (San Francisco: Barry, 1891).

13. This is likely a reference to Franz Schubert's "Ständchen" (Serenade) in *Schwanengesang*, D 957.

14. Worcester refers to William Tecumseh Sherman, who became both famous (and infamous) for his destruction of Southern plantations while marching through Georgia and the Southeast in 1864.

15. Worcester and Bernice Gertrude Beede married in a ceremony held at a private residence on May 22, 1889. The *Carbonate Weekly Chronicle* reported on the surprise wedding on June 3. "The marriage . . . caused a noticeable ripple of excitement in society circles, for it was not altogether expected. The wedding was a quiet one, a few intimate friends of the contracting parties being present." Their first child, Herbert, was born four and a half months later, on October 7. With this "not altogether expected" wedding and Herbert's birthdate in mind, it seems probable that an unplanned pregnancy hastened the nuptials. (It is also rare that Worcester, who had been active with his father in the Presbyterian church, would not have married there.) Considering the common code of honor in late-nineteenth-century America, the marriage would have protected Worcester, and especially Gertrude, from potential social consequences, though they were "two [of the] more popular young people in the city." In this light, the abrupt decision to move first to Denver and then to Pueblo, where Herbert was born, in search of jobs makes more sense. "Worcester-Beede," *Carbonate Weekly Chronicle*, June 3, 1889, 4; Certificate of Marriage #75641, filed May 25, 1889, Lake County Clerk and Recorder's Office, Leadville, CO. My thanks to Fran Masterson for assistance in locating the certificate. Interestingly, in the 1910 U.S. Census, taken in April, Herbert is counted twice in Valparaiso, Indiana. In one entry, taken at college with other students, where it is likely Herbert provided his own information, his correct age of twenty was listed. When recorded at his home address (where Gertrude would have been), he is listed as nineteen years old.

16. Worcester is describing Edward Holden, E. L. Newhouse, and the Philadelphia Smelting and Refining Company of Pueblo, which was soon controlled by the Guggenheims. See Henry Dudley Teetor, "Smelting and Refining in Colorado: Edward Royal Holden," *Magazine of Western History* 10, no. 1 (May 1889), 65–69; "American Smelting v. Bunker Hill: Abstract of Affidavit by E. L. Newhouse," *Mining and Scientific Press* 115, no. 22 (December 1, 1917), 797.

17. Creede first boomed in 1892 and 1893 with the discovery of silver and the Holy Moses Mine. It has been memorialized as one of the last wild boomtowns of the West. Mumey described it: "The silence of the mountains and the ravines was broken by the noise of the pick and shovel, for many came to get rich by their toil, but others planned to separate those fortunate ones from their fortunes." Nolie Mumey, *Creede: History of a Colorado Silver Mining Town* (Denver, CO: Artcraft, 1949), 2; See also Richard C. Huston, *A Silver Camp Called Creede: A Century of Mining* (Montrose, CO: Western Reflections, 2005), and Leland Feitz, *A Quick History of Creede: Colorado Boom Town* (Little London Press, 1983).

18. The silver camp of Creede languished in part because of national and international politics, and especially due to financial debates in the 1890s. The question of gold and silver backing of currency—which had long divided farmers, miners, and bankers—came to a crisis point when the Panic of 1893 hit the financial markets. In response to railroad failures and runs on banks, President Grover Cleveland successfully repealed the Sherman Silver Purchase Act of 1890, which had created artificial demand for the mineral. Without this mandated government purchasing of silver, its prices fell and further constrained investments around Creede.

19. Jefferson Randolph ("Soapy") Smith was born in Georgia in 1860 but became known for his moblike corruption and involvement in local politics in Leadville, Creede, Denver, and then Skagway, Alaska. He arrived in Leadville in 1892, and his most recent biographer, Catherine Holder Spude, writes, "Every place he went, he earned a reputation for petty con games and graft—ameliorated by an indubitable charm." *That Fiend in Hell: Soapy Smith in Legend* (Norman: University of Oklahoma Press, 2012), 5.

3

Colorado, 1893–1905

ABOUT THIS TIME MY OLD FRIEND OF THE BLUE RIBBON Comedy Company who had been working for the smelter in Pueblo got a job as assayer at the Little Jonny Mine, about six miles from Leadville, at an altitude of 12,500 feet above sea level, almost at timber line. He had to have a helper, and offered me the job, and said he would teach me assaying, if I accepted. It only paid three dollars a day, against four dollars on the pump job, but I thought it was a good chance, so I quit the pump job and went with him. It was summer, and the days were long. We did not have to get to work very early, and usually finished about one o'clock, never later than four o'clock in the afternoon, so for several weeks we walked back and forth to work.

On the slope of Breece Hill, a mile or so toward town from the mine, the little sweet wild strawberries were thick, so we often stopped to gather some along the way to take home. I do not know of anything edible that grows at such a high altitude as this, except the delicious wild raspberries that grow in the big rock slides, and which the bears love. There are no truck gardens around Leadville, the season free from frost being far too short. Everything to eat must come from outside. Potatoes that sell for thirty-five cents a hundred pounds in the San Luis Valley bring two dollars a hundred pounds in Leadville.

For a time things went well at the Little Jonny, and they made money. Then the ore pinched down. They used up the funds in the treasury and had to go down into their pockets to keep the mine going. They had about thirty-five men working, driving four headings on the 400-foot level, looking for ore but getting little, and it got down to where, with thirty to thirty-five samples a day, we would have only two or three that were pay ore. One morning about the end of the year the superintendent came in and said, "Well, boys, another week will tell the tale. Absalom is crying and wringing his hands, and says he won't put up any more money." Absalom was a local banker, and he and another of the bank's officials owned 25 percent of the Little Jonny stock. Things went along as they had been for three days, then on the fourth day all four of those drifts broke into good ore, and there seemed to be no end to it. There came a time when, from the output of that body of ore Little Jonny paid monthly dividends of $333,333.33 for several years. There was always some very rich gold ore in the mine, in addition to the silver, lead, and copper that it produced. When I was there, there was a soft gray flat streak on the three-hundred-foot level which was sometimes worth $1,000 a sack, sometimes not more than $50 per ton, so the ore produced on each shift was stacked in sacks in the hoist house by itself until the assays were out, so they could tell what to do with it.

One night two men drove up in a wagon, held up the hoistman, who was alone, and took the pile in one corner. It was worthless to them, as it was only about $50 a ton stuff, while the pile in another corner was $1,000 a sack stuff. Some years after I left there, two leasers working the mine found one slab of gold that brought about $35,000.

After I had worked there for about a year I got the promise of the job of assayer at a mine near town that had never had its own assayer. It was a good job, $150 a month, to take in all the outside work offered, and keep all the money for it. I knew that the outside would bring in at least $200 a month and might amount to as much as $700. I was to report for duty on July 1, 1893. It was to be a good assay office and well equipped, and I was to oversee its building and fitting up, so that it would suit me. So I broke in another man at the Jonny, and quit the job there on June 30. That very same day every mine in the Leadville district, more than a hundred in all, shut down, and the smelters closed as soon as they smelted the ore they had on hand. The Indian mints had stopped coining silver, and as they were the largest steady buyers, the price took a great slump, and it seemed likely that it would never recover. It was a greater calamity than a fire, which wiped out the whole town, would have been. There was no place to look for work, as the whole country was suffering from the great "panic," the other mining camps were as badly off as we, and the rest of the population of Colorado depended almost wholly on the output of the mines.[1]

What to do? My wife's uncle came to the rescue. He was an old time placer miner, having lived and placer-mined for gold in California Gulch, on the slope of which Leadville is built, long before the Leadville boom started. He had just taken a lease on a placer mine about ten miles north of town, and he took me in with him. That was backbreaking work, pick-pick-picking with bended back to help the water wash down the bank, lifting big boulders out of the pit or forking little boulders out of the tail-sluice, or cleaning up bedrock and shoveling gravel off the bedrock into the cleanup sluice. For a while I had about all I could do.

That was the year of the Chicago World's Columbian Exposition, and the G.A.R. had decided that the Drum Corps should make a big showing there in September, when the G.A.R. National Encampment was to be held there.[2] For putting them in shape to make a splurge, and going with them, I was to get $300 and my wife's expenses for the trip in addition to my own. So five evenings a week I rode horseback to drill the Drum Corps, and got up at five o'clock in the morning to be at the mine in time to commence work at seven. After a time, the G.A.R. found that, with money so scarce, it would be impossible to raise funds for the Chicago trip, so the idea was abandoned, and my wife and I did not go to the fair, and I did not get my $300.

Then we took our families out to the mine. My partner had two big boys who each did a man's work in the mine, and a daughter nearly grown besides his wife, and we had three little children. There was a big log house on the mine, big enough for all of us, so we all stayed there together. A pack rat had a nest in one corner just under the eaves, and we often saw and heard him scuttling around, but he seldom took anything from us. Tennessee Gulch, where the mine is, is beautiful in the summertime, with trees and shrubbery and flowers and the clear stream hurrying down. This is a region of plentiful moisture, so the vegetation is luxuriant, and I have never seen elsewhere such an abundance and variety of wild flowers. In front of the house was a thicket of roses, a mass of flowers all over the outside. The gulch is the beginning of the Arkansas River, others uniting with it to form the river, which flows, a clear, cold trout stream down the wide valley below Leadville. There were many porcupines and groundhogs and bushytailed rats, and the usual small life of the woods, with many song birds, and the bears came in the fall to eat the raspberries that grew in a big rockslide above the house. We got enough berries to supply jam for both our families for a year, and one of the boys almost ran into a big cinnamon bear that was eating berries, so he retired rather hastily. The bushes grow in the crevices among the big jagged rocks, which keep them warm through the late summer nights until they can ripen.

On the first pit that we worked out on the mine we made only about fifty cents a day each, but after that we did better, and by the time the water froze up in October we were making about three dollars a day. There were two things that worked against us: there were many big boulders, and we had a bad bedrock. The bedrock was quartzite in thin layers, the top one being only about four inches thick, and seamed in two directions nearly at right angles to each other, so that it was broken into oblong blocks about the size and shape of bricks. The water level was just at the bottom of that first layer. Most of the gold was pretty coarse, so sometimes we would see a bright flake in the water, scurrying for a crevice in the bedrock like a live thing; but if we took up the bedrock to get the gold in those fissures, we were in the water, and the gold was gone.

Finally the water froze up about October first, and we went back to town.[3] My wife's aunt said, "I know where there is a job for you. They want a man to teach in the high school." I said, "I couldn't teach school. It is thirteen years since I finished high school, and I have forgotten most of the little I knew." But she said, "I know that you can teach school if you try, and the school board will give you that job if you ask for it." With little hope of getting the job, I started out to see the members of the school board. As soon as I breached the subject, each of them said, "Why, you're just the one we want. You can handle those boys down there." For five years they had had a woman principal and all women teachers in the high school, and they were having difficulty in maintaining discipline among the larger pupils. So the board decided to get a man teacher to discipline the big boys. On account of the Drum Corps my reputation as a rigid disciplinarian was high. Some of those boys in the high school were Drum Corps boys, and would make no difficulty.

There was one requisite: the teacher must be acquainted with the so-called "continental" pronunciation of Latin. The principal, who was doing the Latin teaching, had convinced the board that it was the only correct one. Fortunately I knew it, so I said I would get a temporary teacher's certificate from the county superintendent, and would take the examination when he held the next one. But they said that they proposed to examine me themselves, as the law allowed them to do, for they had little respect for the county superintendent, and wanted to be sure that I was competent, especially with regard to the Latin pronunciation. I said that I needed a week to rub up for the examination, and they said, "Take all the time you want." I dug up my old school text-books and some others, and burned the midnight oil for a week, cramming for the examination. The committee to examine me consisted of the president, a lawyer and one of the large shareholders of the Little Jonny, who was reputed to be a Latin scholar, and another member who had been county judge, and so was commonly addressed as "Judge," both of them good friends of mine. On the appointed evening

I took my books to the judge's office for my examination. Said the judge to the other man, "You know this Latin is the most important thing, Charley, and you are the Latin scholar, so you examine him first in that." But Charley said, "I'll tell you Judge, I've just about forgotten all the Latin I ever knew. I couldn't conjugate a Latin verb to save my soul. I am not competent to examine him." So they decided to try something else, and it being the judge's turn, he thumbed two or three of the text-books, and then he said, "Now, Charley, this is all foolishness. Len has just been studying these things, and knows ten times as much about them as we do, so what is the use of us trying to examine him? We know him. If he says he can teach these things, he can do it, so let's put him to work."[4]

I reported to the Principal for duty, and she asked, "What do you prefer to teach?" I said, "You can give me anything you please except algebra, which I hate and will not teach." She loved algebra and was teaching it, so that just suited her. She gave me eight studies, so I would be hearing recitations steadily all day long. Until three o'clock I heard them in the office in the basement, which was easy enough, but for the last hour of the day I had charge of a big room with almost a hundred pupils in it, maintaining order and hearing recitations at the same time.

As expected, some of the larger boys decided that I should be shown what was what, and one of them started the affair when I told him to come and sit in a front seat for making a noise. He stood up and said, "You nor anyone like you can make me do that." I started for him, but he was nearer the door than I, and escaped. Next morning I was waiting for him at the top of the big stairway when school opened. He was the last one in the line that came up the stairway. I said, "Come down to the office, I want to talk to you." He pulled a buggy spoke from under his coat and made a pass at me and turned and ran down stairs with me after him. I caught him at the foot of the stairs, and down he went, with me on top of him. I took the buggy spoke and beat him well with it, he all the time yelling at the top of his voice.

Colorado

It seems that the other boys were to come to his assistance, if he got into difficulty and called for them, but the principal was game and backed up against the closed door, and told them to keep their seat when they started to get up, and they subsided. Then I did something I could not have done except under the influence of excitement. I picked him up, and carried him, still yelling, out the front door and down the steps into the basement and set him in a chair. His father was a blacksmith, a big man, with a shop almost directly across the street from the front door of the school. Just as I set the boy down in the chair, the father burst into the room in his leather apron and with a hammer in his hand, and shouted that he was going to have a hand in the affair. I was pretty badly scared, but I told him that he could not make any such talk as that in that office, but to sit down and I would tell him all about it, and then we could decide what to do. When he found out what had happened, and I said the boy had got just what was coming to him, and would come to any boy that tried to make trouble in that school, he agreed with me, and we parted friends, he taking the boy to get cleaned up and sent back at recess time, and nothing further to be said.

When the other boys in the plot heard what had happened, they decided on reprisals, and ambushed me when I came back from lunch, behind a high board fence, near the back door of the school house, but, when the time came for them to issue from ambush, their hearts failed them. I had a drumstick in my overcoat pocket, with which to defend myself in ease of trouble, and the sight of that may have influenced them. None of the Drum Corps boys were involved in the uprising.

I got along better with the teaching than I expected. I didn't mind the teaching itself so much, but having to maintain order at the same time irked me. My salary was twenty dollars a week, on which I could live, and I was certainly glad to get it. The county supported five hundred families through that winter, of men who usually made a good living. Among the studies which I taught was English literature, and I found out something about the literary tastes of seventeen-year-old boys and girls. I think that none of them cared much for the "classics." It was hard to drag them through *Paradise Lost*, and Shakespeare was little better. The most popular author of all was John Bunyan.[5]

Toward the end of the term, the president of the school board came and asked me if I thought I would like to make teaching my profession. I said no, that I had only taken the job to keep from starving, and would give it up as soon as I could get something else to do. He said they had been watching me, and they liked my work, and they had decided to go back to the system which had been followed for a long time, until five years before, of having a city superintendent of schools. If I thought I should like to make teaching my profession, he thought the board might offer me the job at $2,000 a year with the customary three months vacation. That was a lot of money, under the circumstances, and I was much tempted to say that I would consider it, if they should offer it to me. The man who took it went from there to a $5,000 job, and held that class of jobs until last year, when he retired and went to live in southern California.

When school closed in the spring, I took an agency to sell bonds of a New York real estate company, my territory to be the City and County of Pueblo, Colorado. It looked like a good investment to me, and I thought I could sell a lot of the bonds. I had not yet found out that as a salesman I had no ability whatsoever. So I set out hopefully for Pueblo.

About this time a long-continued strike of miners at the new mining camp of Cripple Creek had reached an acute stage, and the sheriff of that county was recruiting deputies by the hundreds to march on the headquarters of the strikers and make wholesale arrests.[6] Among these deputies was a troop of sixty-five from Leadville, under the leadership of the clerk of the district court, a chum of mine. They had left in a special car for Colorado Springs a few days before I left for Pueblo, but had been held up by railroad washouts at Salida, so that I arrived at Pueblo almost immediately after they did. When the leader saw me going through the station gate, he caught up with me and clapped me on the shoulder, saying, "What are you doing here? You've got to go with us." And he would not take no for an answer.

I got on the car with him, and the men all knowing me, I received a cordial welcome. We were taken to Colorado Springs and sworn in as deputy sheriffs, and each given a rifle and ammunition, and that evening we left on a freight train for the terminus of the railroad building toward Cripple Creek. We carried a six-inch rifled field gun with its caisson and ammunition, and a four-horse team carried a new Gatling rapid-fire gun, still in the boxes, with its caisson and ammunition. A two-horse team took all the rest of the munitions and supplies for a thousand or more deputy sheriffs without training or instructions. The Gatling gun was turned over to our company, and I was made a member of its crew as a powder monkey, and given a six-shooter in place of the rifle I had. We unpacked the gun and set it up on the wheels on the train, and we filled the caisson with ammunition.

Arriving at the terminus about daybreak, in a pouring rain which had been falling all night, we set forth to march to Beaver Park, ten miles away and about five miles from Cripple Creek, but within sight of Altman, the town on top of Bull Hill, which the strikers made their headquarters, where we went into camp. In the afternoon the Colorado National Guard in large force marched past our camp and made camp farther down the park, between us and Cripple Creek. In the morning there was about four inches of snow on the ground, but the sun came out bright and warm, and it soon began to melt rapidly. After breakfast we were formed into three detachments, to approach the stronghold of the strikers, the Pharmacist Mine at Altman, from three directions. When our forty or fifty mounted men went over toward Bull Hill to round up their horses, some strikers hidden in the timber on the slope of the hill began shooting at them. The cannon was limbered up and went down there on the run, and planted a couple of shells on the hillside, and we could see the strikers hurrying along the slope among the trees.

Then we started for Altman. Our detachment was made up of the Leadville contingent and that from the town of Cripple Creek, about 115 altogether, in charge of Bob Mullen, the undersheriff, who had about three hundred warrants to serve on the strikers.[7] The sheriff stayed in camp, and we jeered at him as we filed past his tent, and sang, "The sheriff of El Paso he had a thousand men, He marched them up the hill and he marched them down again." When we were about half-way to Altman a horseman overtook us with a message from the sheriff for Mullen, telling him that we were nearly surrounded, and must return immediately to camp, but Mullen ignored it, and we proceeded. When we reached the summit of Hoosier Pass, which leads down to Cripple Creek, and where the road branches off up the hill to Altman, there was the militia, drawn up across the road to Altman, with machine guns planted to cover it. General Brooks, in command, called upon us to halt, and said that if we took another step toward Altman, he would open fire upon us. The governor of Colorado, Waite, had announced that he would protect the strikers, even though it should be necessary to wade in blood to the horses' bridles, and Brooks had instructions from him to act accordingly.[8] So after some heated discussion, Mullen gave it up, and we marched down the hill to Cripple Creek, then through the heart of the district to the other end, and made camp at Stratton's Independence Mine.

The leader of the Leadville contingent was a colonel on the governor's staff, and as soon as General Brooks saw him, he ordered him to immediately take his place in the militia, or he would have him arrested and court-martialed. So he turned over his command to me, and joined Brooks. In the meantime the leaders of the strikers at Altman had announced to them that the "jig was up," and advised them to go home and hide their guns and be good. Then they mounted their horses and left for parts unknown, and the strike was over. The next day we marched back to the railroad and took the train to Colorado Springs, where we were dismissed. I received thirty dollars for my services, which was a help, as I had borrowed fifty dollars from the janitor of the school when I left for Pueblo.

In Pueblo I soon found out what a poor salesman I was. I couldn't sell perfectly good prospects who had money to invest and only wanted to be sure that the security was all right. After a few days, in which I failed to make a single sale, the assayer in whose office I made my hang-out told me that the superintendent of the Pueblo Smelting & Refining Company needed an assayer right away, and wanted me to come and see him. I was not quite ready to give up the bond business, so I did not go, but the next day he left word again for me to come and see him. I did so, and he offered me the job of ore assayer. I told him I had never assayed for a smelter, and I was afraid I might not be able to handle the work to his satisfaction. He said, "You know how to make assays for gold, silver, and lead don't you?" I said, "Yes." He said, "That's all I want."

I went to work right away, and found it not as difficult as I had feared. That smelter was quite a concern, with lead and copper furnaces and a lead and silver refiner, and they produced some antimony, which they saved from the dross in the lead refinery. The superintendent was a metallurgical genius, and was always finding new ways to improve the smelting and refining methods. After a long and successful career, during which he was for a time superintendent of the greatest smelter in the world—where he revolutionized the blast-furnace smelting of copper and later received a salary from the Guggenheims said to be $100,000 a year—he is teaching mine management at the University of Arizona.

Every day while I was working there, a big two-horse express wagon came and hauled away twenty thousand ounces of silver-gold bullion from the refinery. It had a high proportion of gold, as we were getting a lot of high-grade gold ore from Cripple Creek by that time. After a few months I had a chance to go to Cripple Creek to assay for a mine there, which would pay me at least twice as much as I was getting from the smelter, so of course I went.

It was hard to find a house in Cripple Creek. Things were on the boom there then, and almost every day newcomers would stop me on the street to ask if I knew where they could find a place to sleep. I finally got a good log house with a lean-to kitchen, four rooms in all, in a good neighborhood. The mine was about five miles away, so I had to go horseback to and fro over the hills to work. After some years a trolley loop line was built through the district, which, with three railroads running frequent suburban trains, provided ample passenger service to all the mines, so I did not need the horse any more. Soon after I went there a man came to me and said that he represented people in Denver who wished to buy the mine where I worked; that they already had sufficient information about the mine so that they did not need to make an examination, and were ready to pay $600,000 cash for it, and would give me a commission of $60,000, if I could secure the mine for them at that price.

So the next time the president and vice president came up from Manitou I told them about the offer, but they said, "You may tell anyone that talks to you about buying this mine that it is not for sale at any price." I said, "Do you mean to say that if somebody came along and offered you $10 million for the mine, you would not accept it?" They said, "No." I said, "Why not? The mine is not worth anything like $600,000. You are taking the ore out as fast as you are developing it, so that you have almost no ore in reserve, and there is no telling when the ore may play out." But they said, "We figure that if the mine is worth any price to anyone else, it is worth more than that to us." There was no use arguing against such reasoning, so I gave it up, but I told them I was afraid they would be sorry they did not sell when they could. A few months after that the ore values petered out almost without warning, and they spent more than they had made out of the mine, looking for more ore. When they gave it up, and stopped work on the mine, I rented the assay office and used it as a custom office.

One day in the Spring of 1897[9] the manager of the mine came in and said that someone had just telephoned that there was a big fire in Cripple Creek, and the blaze seemed to be going toward my house, so I had better be getting home. I caught my horse and set forth as quickly as I could. When I got in sight of town, there were several blocks of buildings afire, and I had to make a long detour to get home, which was right in the path of the fire. I found friends already there to help me move out with two wagons, which some of them commandeered and were holding for me. They were sure the fire would come and burn my house. We set to, and hustled everything out, and sent it off. The fire came up the hill to the other side of the street, but they blew up the houses there, and it did not cross the street. One load of my household goods got back that evening, but the other did not return until the next day. The fire burned about half the town, and a week from that day, at just the same hour, another fire started which wiped out nearly all the rest. I went through the same performance as I had for the other fire, with the same result. The fire did not touch the block on which I lived, although it burned three of the blocks surrounding it. I have a photograph of that fire, taken at its height from the schoolhouse just above my house. The principal of that school at that time is now the manager of the city-county hospital and the county poor farm here in El Paso.

When we first went there, my wife and I joined a Congregational church which held its services in a big tent, and when they found that she could play the organ and that I had some experience as a choir singer, they asked her to be the organist and me to take charge of the choir, which we did without remuneration. They were building a church, and had it almost finished, enough so that they were using it for services, when the fire came along and burned it down. Someone had donated a fine big bell, and the sexton rang the bell until the fire drove him away.

Soon after I arrived at the assay office of the mine on my first morning there, a man came with some samples, and introduced himself as the manager of the adjoining property. They had a big vein on their ground and had done a lot of work looking for ore, but had never had a pay assay. He said, "There is just one result I will not accept, and that is two dollars and forty cents. I am fed up with $2.40 assays, and I refuse to accept anymore." I said that thereafter when I got a $2.40 result, I would call it $2.50. They worked there almost continuously, and I made their assays as long as I was in Cripple Creek, more than ten years, and they got their first pay assay shortly before I left there. From that time on their fortunes improved, and that mine is still paying regular monthly dividends, having been to date the greatest producer in the district. It once shipped one trainload of ore that net more than $1 million.

The richest lot of ore in large quantity that I have ever known of was a sixty-ton lot shipped to the smelter in Denver by the Isabella Mine on Bull Hill. There was some difficulty in getting the assays of the smelter and the mine to agree. So they agreed to take a new sample and submit it to five different assayers, settlement to be made on the average of the five results. I was the highest, 512 ounces gold per ton. The lowest was 510 ounces, and the average a little over 511 ounces, or approximately $10,220 a ton at the much lower value of gold of that time. I have melted gold out of ore there that was worth sixty dollars a pound.

Cripple Creek was a "poor man's camp." Very rich ore was sometimes found at the "grassroots," and I know of two mines where the soil was shoveled up with horse scrapers, and shipped to the smelter. There was so much very rich ore that it was estimated that at least $100,000 worth was stolen every month. Many poor men who knew nothing about mining got rich there. Experienced prospectors and miners and mining engineers shunned it at first, thinking there was nothing there, so most of the claims were taken up by "hay shovelers" from the drought ridden dust bowl of western Kansas and eastern Colorado, which was having its first prolonged drought.

The one who made the most money was a carpenter from Colorado Springs.[10] He shut up his shop for the summer, and went off prospecting to Cripple Creek, with a buckboard and a pair of ponies. When he found that practically all the ground near town had already been taken up, he went off five or six miles, where there was plenty of free ground, and located a couple of claims on the Fourth of July, which he called the "Independence" and "Martha Washington," and started in doing his assessment work. One evening when he went home from work he took a chunk of rock, from a big rotten-granite dike that stuck above the surface on his ground, to the assayer, who gave him high values. He thought the assayer had made a mistake, but when he took a larger sample the next time, the assayer gave him even better results than before. So he began breaking down the dike and shipping it to the smelter, and sinking a shaft on it. After he had made about three million dollars working the mine, he sold it to a British corporation for ten million dollars, incidentally helping another man to make a fortune.

He had a neighbor in Colorado Springs, a literary man, who I imagine was none too prosperous, and as it was understood that all offers to buy the mine had been refused, this corporation approached the literary neighbor with a proposition to try to get an option on the mine, for which, if he succeeded, they would pay him $600,000. After he got his commission, he joined with some other Colorado Springs men who had made money in Cripple Creek in the organization of an oil company, which was immensely profitable. A year or two ago I saw a notice of his death, with an estimated fortune of $20 million.

The purchase of the mine was made on the recommendation of a famous British mining engineer. Later some of the stockholders of the new corporation became apprehensive that the mine would never repay what had been paid for the stock, and engaged a famous American engineer to examine it for them, and he reported that he believed that it would never pay back in dividends the ten million that had been paid for it. So the stockholders sued the British corporation, and the engineers who made the examination for the suit sent me the samples for assay. Every day I had to go with a wagon to the Independence shaft, and wait until the engineers came up with the samples in sealed sacks, and take them to my assay office two or three miles away. They took big samples, and many of them, so I must have had two or three tons of ore from that lot. I do not remember how that suit came out, but I think the mine finally paid in dividends more than was paid for it.

One day the engineer for whom I had worked in Leadville, and who had moved to Cripple Creek, called me up and asked me if I would like to go to Mexico to help him examine a mine and make the assays there. I had never been in Mexico, and was much pleased to have the chance. I had to take a complete assay outfit with me, and enough supplies to make a lot of assays, which I packed in four trunks, so that I could take it all right along with me.[11] We went to the City of Chihuahua by train, and there we found a guide, philosopher, and friend awaiting us in the person of an Italian-Mexican from Arizona, who went by the name of "Pilón" (bald). He had been sent in advance, and had pack-mules and *mozos* and everything for the trip ready at the end of the railroad 125 miles west of Chihuahua, and went with us from there.

The mine was three days mule-back from the end of the railroad, in the Sierra Madre Mountains, but Pilón took such good care of us that we suffered no discomfort except the soreness from the mule-back riding. The mine was not merely a mine, it was a great mining concession of 45,000 hectares, about 112,000 acres, as big as the whole Cripple Creek district, crisscrossed with veins, with several shafts from which gold-silver ore was being extracted and treated in a stamp mill. There was a well-equipped assay office at the mill, so I did not need mine, but they had a limited supply of material for assaying, so it was well that I had plenty. I had plenty of helpers, but they spoke no word of English, and I had acquired only a few words of Spanish, such as "*más carbón*" when I wanted more charcoal in the furnace. Even the mill superintendent, who was also the assayer, knew no English, but it is surprising how well you can get along with sign language only, when you have to.

The engineer had only ten days in which to make the examination. He had several men to help him with the sampling underground, and as fast as the samples were taken they were sent to the assay office, so I could get to work on them at once. I did the sampling at the mill while I was making the assays, a set of heads and tails samples every hour of the day while we were there, which I assayed along with the mine samples. That was a very enjoyable trip. Pilón was a very efficient mayordomo.[12] He was the best pistol shot from the back of a horse that I have ever seen. He would pull out his six gun, riding along the trail, and cut off saplings the size of your finger along the trail, without stopping and with hardly ever a miss.

A few weeks after I returned from that trip, a mining promoter in Denver called me one afternoon late, to ask if I would go to Mexico with his engineer, to give him the same kind of assistance as on the former trip. When I assented, he wanted me to meet him in Denver at nine o'clock the next morning. He had to leave for the East at noon, and he wanted to talk to me before he went, and wanted his engineer and me to leave for Mexico the same night. I hurried home from the mine to find that there was no train to Denver, both roads which had night trains having been washed out by a big storm that day. Then I learned that the D.&R.G. Railroad also had a washout east of Leadville and was sending its through-trains from the west from Leadville by the Colorado Midland through Cameron, a station five miles from Cripple Creek. Three trains were expected about nine o'clock that night at Cameron. I took the trolley to Windy Point on Bull Hill and carried my luggage down the dark steep hill through the wet pine woods to Cameron, and boarded a train. When the conductor spotted me, I told him I was going to Denver. He said he could not take me, but we were already on the way, and when I explained that I had to be in Denver the next morning, and there was no other way to get there, he relented, and with the consent of the Short Line conductor who was traveling with him, took my fare. So I kept my appointment and found that my man was the same one who had been trying to sell the mine that I had been to in Mexico to the people we had been examining it for, the so-called Colorado Mill Trust. I had the same rail trip as before, then five days mule-back to the mine, with Pilón as mayordomo.

The mine was at the village of Dolores, which the Apache chief Geronimo was accustomed to make his retreat between raids, and the salients of the hills around were covered with rock fortifications.[13] He had planted a peach orchard there, and the peaches were just getting ripe, so I had plenty to eat, such as they were. They were of the variety known in Mexico as "*duraznos*," hard, tasteless clingstones.

The assayer at the mine was also the doctor and the Comisario of Police in the village, and was a Mexican of German descent, educated in St. Louis. I formed a lasting friendship with him, which continues until now. He had a home-made assay furnace of firebrick without mortar, and a gasoline burner to heat the muffle. It worked very well, but after a few days, supplies being detained by storms, the gasoline played out, and I had to fall back on an old charcoal furnace in an adobe hut, with a leaky roof that made the dirt floor a quagmire. To keep up with the sampling, I had to get to work at daylight, and work until I could no longer see. This was a good mine, gold and silver, which had been bought from its original Mexican owners by some California mining men and a Scotchman. The ore had to be packed on mules to the railroad, which took ten days, then 350 miles by rail to the El Paso smelter. They shipped only ore which had a value of $100 or more a ton.

We were about a month making the examination, when our employer came along. He had an option of $1,650,000 on the mine, which was about to expire. But we found ore which we estimated to be worth net only $1,250,000. They would not extend the time of his option, to give him a chance to develop more ore, nor accept $1,250,000, which he offered them for the mine. So he lost his option, and they later sold the mine to another party for the same price he had offered them.

We went to the mine I had been to on my former trip, and I made another set of assays there. My employer later sold that mine to a well-known oil man, and he worked it for some years, until revolutionists drove his men away.

In Chihuahua, where I waited for my employer two or three

days while he finished some business, it seemed that all the old surreys and chaises from the U.S. had been assembled around the main plaza, hitched up to a lot of decrepit old horses that had to lean against each other when they trotted. Pilón hired one of these "coaches," and took me on a tour of the sights. One of these was the "*Plaza de Gallos*," the cock-fighting ring, where, when we went in, they were doing the preliminary betting on a bout between a fine red Spanish fighting cock and a big fat Dominick rooster, and it seemed that every man there wanted to bet with us against the Dominick. Just to show that I was a good fellow, I bet a peso for myself and one for Pilón on the Dominick, which squatted down when the red chicken flew at it and with one pass almost cut the other chicken in two. They do not use spurs, but gaffs like miniature razors.

When I got home from that trip, I found that I did not have any assay office. The man who had been the assayer there before I went there, and who got me the place when he left there, decided that he wanted the office again, and prevailed the company to throw out the man I had left in charge. It was a good thing for me, as the mine which had the best assay office in the Cripple Creek district needed an assayer, and I leased their assay office for a nominal rental with a contract to do their assaying.

About this time an old customer, for whom I had done some favors, the superintendent of a mine on Bull Hill, came to me and said, "We have made a wonderful strike at our place, and have kept it quiet, but of course it will get out pretty soon. If you want to make a killing, buy all the Acacia stock you can. It is fifty cents now, and it will sure go to at least a dollar as soon as this gets out." I borrowed all the money I could and bought all the stock it would buy on a 10 percent margin, at fifty cents a share.

That very day the big slump struck the Cripple Creek Stock Exchange, and everything went to pieces, and almost all the brokers went broke, along with their customers. I had very good credit, and the brokers with whom I dealt thought it was only a flurry. They had a good deal of cash on hand, so they did not sell me out until they had to do it. By that time I owed them a

lot of money. I made an arrangement to pay in monthly install-
ments, which I did for two or three years, when I managed to
get a loan from a bank, and paid them off. I was almost ten years
getting that debt paid off, ten years during which every cent I
could rake and scrape had to go for interest and principal on
that debt. I shall never forget the day I made the last payment
on it: Christmas Day, 1909.

Just at the time I made that bad investment, a woman whose
husband was one of my first acquaintances in Leadville, a hoistman at the Portland Mine in Cripple Creek and who was singing in my choir, told me she had saved $100 from the money
her husband gave her to run the household with, without his
knowledge, and she wanted me to invest it in mining stocks for
her. She had heard that I was quite a wizard as a stock operator, and never made a mistake. I very reluctantly consented,
and told her about a stock I was just buying for myself, and
that I would buy some of that for her, and asked her whether I
should margin it or not. She wanted to make as much as possible, so she said to margin it, which I did, and the slump wiped
her out. Then she came and tearfully demanded her money
back, although I had tried to impress upon here that I would
not be responsible in case of loss. When I declined to pay, she
told her husband, who angrily demanded restitution, and made
a lot of nasty talk. So I paid the $100, and I have shunned busi-
ness with women ever since.

Soon after this, there was a general strike in the mines by
the miners' union, which demanded that only union miners
be employed, and that the employers collect the dues for the
union from the miners.[14] The mines refused. They were all working union hours and paying union wages, and made no dis-
crimination against union men. All the principal mines closed
down, but I kept my assay office open, as I had many customers who were leasers, not affected by the strike, many of them
being union men. There was a good deal of trouble and violence, and twenty or more men were murdered by strikers, and
a lot of militia were sent to try and keep order.[15]

The Mine Owners' and Operators' Association formed an organization called the Citizens' Alliance, which I joined, to fight the strike. The Citizen's Alliance proceeded to deport strikers by ones and twos and squads up to twenty or so, and finally rounded up some two hundred at once, and put them on a special train and shipped them under guard to Kansas.

The man to whom I had refunded that money was one of those deported. He went to Denver, and after some time he got a job as engineer of an office building there, and set forth one morning to walk down town to start on his new job. He took a path across a vacant lot, where the notorious Harry Orchard had planted a bomb to blow up one of the justices of the State Supreme Court, who went that way every morning down to the State House. He picked up the bomb, and was blown to bits. The same Orchard blew up a suburban train loaded with non-striking miners going to work, and killed fourteen of them. The strikers lost out, and from that time on no man could get work in the Cripple Creek mines without a card from the Mine Owners' and Operators' Association.

An assayer friend of mine, who had made some money out of the sale of a mine, told me he was going to Chihuahua to live, and contemplated establishing an assay office there, as a headquarters where he might secure information about mines and prospects, which he might secure under option, and carry on a mine brokerage business. The assay office is the information bureau of the mining business. He did not want to run the assay office himself, only to have it for a headquarters, and asked me if I would run it for him, when he got ready. It was evident to me that Cripple Creek, like all mining camps, must have passed the peak of its production, and that I should have to be moving, probably in the not far distant future. I was tired of the high altitudes and long cold winters of the Colorado mining camps, and thought I should prefer the climate of Chihuahua, which is the center of a great mining region, where I might establish a permanent assay business not dependent on the output of a single mining camp. I said yes. Now he wired me that he was ready for me to come and take a look, which I did.

He proposed that he should equip the assay office and finance it until it should be self-sustaining, that each month I should take the first $150 profits, if they amounted to that much, as my salary, and any profits above that amount should be divided equally between us. I agreed to this, provided that I should have entire charge of the business, and he should have nothing whatever to say about running it. He assented to this, and so, without any written agreement, our partnership began, and lasted for more than ten years, until I was forced by the revolutions to leave the country, during which we never had a disagreement nor a harsh word spoken, and he received as his share of the profits more than twelve times the amount of his investment.

Of course, I hated to leave Cripple Creek after so many years of pleasant residence, and my wife was even more reluctant than I. I owned my house and furniture, and my business was still fairly prosperous. The mine whose assay office I was using was a model mine. I have never seen another mine where all the equipment was so up-to-date and so efficiently handled. From boiler room to the bottom of the mine, everything was spick and span. Visitors went down in the mine without changing clothes or donning overalls, and came out with them spotless.

I should have made a fortune by that time, with all the opportunities I had had, but although I had mined most of the time, I had been there in a small way. I was just about even with the game. Sometimes I made a little money, and sometimes I lost a little. Perhaps I was too cautious. Practically all men who live in mining camps do some mining on their own account, no matter what their avocation. It may be only buying mining stock, but none of them escapes participation in the mining business.

I barely missed making my fortune just before I left there. On one of the claims of the company where I was assaying, there was an altered granite dike averaging about fifteen feet wide, through which they had run drifts from the shaft every hundred feet down to nine hundred feet from the surface, with track and compressed-air pipe on every level ready to mine the ore. The ore had an average value of eight dollars per ton in gold and there were at least fifty thousand tons exposed on the different levels, and probably many times that much not yet developed. They had sent a carload of the ore to a testing works in Denver, to find out if it could be concentrated profitably, and the president of the company was not pleased with the results, and decided that they would never do anything with the ore. I had experimented with the ore, and believed that it could be easily concentrated, with a saving of at least 80 percent of its gold values, at a total cost of not more than two dollars per ton for mining and milling. I took the engineer for a big mining concern who was looking for something in Cripple Creek down into the mine, and showed him the ore and the results of my experiments. He said they would furnish $40,000 to build a two-hundred-ton a day capacity mill for half the profits, if I could get a lease on the ore on terms which I proposed, and would allow me a salary of $200 a month for managing it. I asked the president of our company, and he said he was willing, and would recommend it to the executive committee at the next meeting. But one member of the committee opposed it. He thought they could some day build a mill, and make a lot of money out of that ore. Some years after, they built the mill and made more than a million dollars off that ore.

The work at Chihuahua would be quite different from what I had been used to, up to that time, which had been almost exclusively assaying for gold, silver, and lead by fire, whereas in Chihuahua I should have varied determinations to make on all sorts of ores and minerals, more of them by wet methods than by fire.

Before I went to Chihuahua, I went to the Colorado School of Mines at Golden, where I had friends among the faculty. The dean of the chemistry department let me use his private laboratory to work in, to get some practice in work with which I was not familiar.[16] What I needed was about a six-month intensive course in metallurgical chemistry, but I could not take more than ten days, so I concentrated on the principal essentials, and trusted to luck to get by with the others that I should have to do. It happened that I had many determinations to make with which I was not familiar. But I had some good books on assaying and chemistry, in which I could find reliable schemes for almost any determination I might have to make. I got by better than might have been expected, and did not expose my ignorance and lack of practice.

Notes

1. On the Panic of 1893, see chap2n18.

2. Scholars often point to the Chicago World's Fair of 1893—the "Columbian" Exposition to celebrate the recent 400th anniversary of Christopher Columbus' landing—as an important turn in American history, not only for the technological advances on display, but also for the presentation of Frederick Jackson Turner. His "Significance of the Frontier to American History" was one of the most influential historical tracts in terms of its lingering interpretive claims: that the frontier advanced American development and was critical to the development of democracy. Scholars now refute this interpretation for its cultural bias and teleological flaws. The Turnerian perspective on the virtues of the frontier (and, by extension, of manifest destiny) would have been the consensus among Anglo-Americans like Worcester at this time. See esp. John Mack Faragher, *Rereading Frederick Jackson Turner: "The Significance of the Frontier in American History" and Other Essays* (New Haven: Yale University Press, 1999), and Richard Etulain, *Does the Frontier Experience Make the West Exceptional?* (Boston: Bedford/St. Martin's, 1999).

3. Leadville.

4. The President of the School Board and part-owner of the Little Jonny Mine was Charles Cavender, and the other member of the committee, "Judge," was likely A. V. Hunter, a former judge of elections. Worcester does not mention that his father had served as secretary of the board for a number of years, as late as 1890, with each of these men. "School Board Meeting," *Herald Democrat*, November 26, 1890, 4. Worcester (Junior) taught in Leadville's Central School in 1893, and his sister, Mabel, taught younger grades for a number of years after 1894.

5. Among other works, Bunyan wrote and is most known for his *Pilgrim's Progress* (1678).

6. The Cripple Creek strike of 1894 was "the only mining strike of the period in which the power of the state protected civil peace rather than mine owners' property." Elizabeth Jameson, *All That Glitters: Class, Conflict, and Community in Cripple Creek* (Urbana: University of Illinois Press, 1998), 6. As a deputy sheriff, willing to quash organized labor resistance, Worcester therefore had joined what would be the losing side of the conflict.

7. Worcester's description of his experience with Bob Mullen in the 1894 strike squares with the account written by John Calderwood, which appeared as historical context in Emma Florence Langdon, *The Cripple Creek Strike, 1903–1904* (Victor CO: n.p., 1904), 38–40. Mullen often appears as "Mullins" in contemporary narratives. B. M. Rastall, *The Cripple Creek Strike of 1893* (Colorado Springs: n.p., 1905), 33.

8. Davis Waite was governor of Colorado from 1893 to 1895.

9. Worcester misidentifies the year. The Cripple Creek fires raged in April 1896.

10. Winfield Scott Stratton.

11. The original line in the manuscript here notes that Worcester packed *five* trunks, but he later refers to them as his "four trunks." Since his descendants still have four large trunks filled with books and papers, the first reference has been amended to four.

12. Mayordomo often translates as "manager," especially of a hacienda, but Worcester uses it more as a referent to "guide" in this instance.

13. Worcester mentions Geronimo, whose capture in 1886 demarcated, for contemporary Americans, the end of the Indian wars. The search for and capture of Geronimo was but one event in a multi-century history of Native American persecution, forced removal, and attempted cultural genocide in the greater West. For recent studies in Geronimo and Apache resistance to U.S. forces in the nineteenth century, see Brian DeLay, *War of a Thousand Deserts: Indian Raids and the U.S.-Mexican War* (New Haven: Yale University Press, 2008); Paul Andrew Hutton, *The Apache Wars: The Hunt for Geronimo, the Apache Kid, and the Captive Boy Who Started the Longest War in American History* (New York: Crown, 2016); and Janne Lahti, *Wars for Empire: Apaches, the United States, and the Southwest Borderlands* (Norman: University of Oklahoma Press, 2017).

14. The Cripple Creek Strike of 1903–1904 resulted in the breaking of the labor union's power.

15. On the strike, see esp. Jameson, *All That Glitters;* and Tim Blevins, Chris Nicholl, and Calvin P. Otto, eds., *The Colorado Labor Wars: Cripple Creek District* (Colorado Springs: Pikes Peak Library District, 2006).

16. No "dean" can be identified for the Chemistry Department at the Colorado School of Mines in 1905, but the only full professor, Dr. Herman Fleck, led the department from 1903 to 1916. My thanks to Ruth Jones and Megan Rose at the School of Mines for their assistance with this inquiry.

4

Borderland Mining and the Early Revolution, 1905–1914

WHEN I ARRIVED IN CHIHUAHUA MY EQUIPMENT AND SUP-plies were already there, but not yet set up. I had three rooms on the ground floor of the principal hotel, which was on the corner of the main plaza. It was a stone building, with walls three feet thick, even the partitions between the rooms, so I could fasten nothing to them without drilling holes into the stone and driving wooden stobs. In spite of that massive construction, there was so much lumber and furniture in the hotel that a few months ago it was destroyed by fire.

Work was already coming in, and the first day a man brought in three big samples of what looked to me like chalky limestone; but he said it was high-grade zinc ore, and he must have his results by noon the next day at the latest. So I said I would get them out for him by that time, and worked until late that night and all the next morning getting things ready and making those zincs. To my great surprise, they showed a high zinc content, and I was afraid I had made some mistake, but it was already noon, so I took the certificate to the man at his hotel, as I had promised, and told him that I feared I had, in my hurried preparations, made some mistake, and would do them over again to make sure. He was not worried, however, saying that he was an old Wisconsin zinc miner and familiar with that kind of ore. He had found a deposit of zinc ore that stuck up high in the air, just the shape of a huge thumb, and he proceeded to knock it down and send it to the smelter.

In addition to assaying I bought zinc ore for a New York company. A few weeks after I went to Chihuahua a Spaniard came in and said he had a big body of high-grade zinc ore on the surface, but that he knew nothing about zinc ore, and [would] much rather lease me the mine than to mine the ore and sell it to me, and offered to lease it to me on a royalty of two dollars per ton. His samples were very good, so I went with him to see the mine, arriving there after an all-day trip by train and wagon. Then he told me that he did not yet have possession of the ground which he intended to lease me, and it was being worked by others. The ground adjoining his was held by the governor of the state, and when he had it surveyed for the title the surveyor had moved one of the monuments so as to include this ground where the ore was located. When he found it out, he complained to the governor, and he agreed to restore the ground in ten days.[1]

The man who had found the ore, who had brought me those first zinc samples, a red-headed Irishman who had lived in Leadville when I lived there, had taken a Scotchman and an American as partners, and they had leased the ground from the governor. The Spaniard was afraid to go over there, so in the morning I went over, and found that the man in charge, the American partner, was an acquaintance. I explained the situation to him, and he said that they did not acknowledge any right which the Spaniard might claim, and I could not take any samples for him, but I could take all the samples I wished for myself, which I did. The Spaniard said that he would make me out the lease as soon as he got the ground back, and I went back to town and left him at his mine. I did not see him for about a month, when I met him on the street, and he said the governor refused to restore his ground. Later the Irishman told me that the Spaniard, instead of restoring the misplaced monument to its original position, had moved it so as to include some of the governor's ground, discovering which, the governor had refused to restore his ground. Soon afterward, the Spaniard found some good zinc ore on his own ground, which he mined himself, and I bought. He finally sold the mine to some French men for $150,000.

My first contract for ore was for three thousand tons of ore guaranteed to contain not less than 55 percent of lead and zinc combined, which I shipped by rail to Tampico, and from there to Antwerp, and up the Rhine to Halberstadt, Germany. Those were the days of Porfirio Díaz, the great statesman of Mexico, and the country was rich and prosperous. Everybody was making money, and the banks were bursting with it, and the government had a surplus in the treasury. Business of every kind was booming, wages were steadily rising, and there was a scarcity of labor, especially in the mining business. With the best mining law in the world, the great mining districts were overrun with engineers looking for mines and prospects for Americans and other foreigners with capital. Almost every rancher in the Sierra Madres was an intermittent prospector, and many of them owned mines or did some mining.

Chihuahua seemed to be just waking up in a business way. There were not a dozen plate glass windows in the city when I went there, but within a year most of the stores and business establishments on the ground floor had them. There were no paved streets, and the street cars were bob-tail burro cars, but they were supplanted after two or three years by a very efficient electric car system.[2]

The Kansas City, Mexico & Orient Railroad was building from Kansas City to Topolobampo, on the Pacific Coast of Sinaloa, Mexico, and it was planned to run a fleet of ships from there to Japan and China, and so shorten the time from New York to the Orient by several days.[3] There were several stretches of the road completed and running regular trains: one from Kansas City to Alpine, Texas, about 600 miles; one from Chihuahua City east toward the U.S. border at Ojinaga, which was afterward extended to Alpine; one from Miñaca, 125 miles west of Chihuahua on the Chihuahua & Pacific Railroad, to Sanchez, about 100 miles west; and one from Culiacan to Topolobampo. They were working on the stretch between these last two, through the wild and picturesque Sierra Madre Mountains, and it would have been a truly scenic line.

It was being promoted by a well-known American railroad promoter, Arthur Stilwell, who would come to Chihuahua with his private car full of prospective investors, and show them around. He had a cabinet organ in his car, and on Sundays held religious services and played the organ and led the singing. It seems that other railroad people and financiers, from whom he expected assistance, opposed the building of this road, so he had difficulty in selling stock or securing funds by borrowing, so the construction proceeded slowly, and the revolutions began before it was finished, and it is still unfinished.

Once I went out to the end of the track east of Chihuahua, to go on to the ranch of Don Demetrio Oaxaca, an Indian, whose hacienda was some forty-five miles beyond the terminal.[4] He and his father and two brothers owned a gold mine not far from there, called "La Virgen," in which the gold was contained in pitchblende, an ore of uranium oxide, a black mineral rich in radium, the gold being the nearest to absolutely pure 1000-fine native gold that I have ever seen, and having assumed the crystalline form of the pitchblende. Don Demetrio's share of the profits from the mine was enough to buy this ranch of more than a hundred thousand acres and improve it. He had three mines on the ranch: one a silver mine, one a lead-silver mine, and the other a copper-silver mine. There was also a hot spring about a half-mile above the hacienda, at the foot of a mountain, where the water did not boil up, as is the usual habit of springs, but flowed gently from a round watercourse in the rock, large enough for a man to crawl into, and ran down past the hacienda, with a volume which I guessed to be about two thousand gallons a minute. By the time it reached the hacienda it had cooled enough so that it was just right for a hot bath, and Don Demetrio had dug a bathing pool, through which the stream ran, and put a house over it. He said he was going to pipe the water into all the rooms of the two big two-story dwelling houses of the hacienda.

Below the bathhouse was a blacksmith shop, with a forge blown by a water blast from the stream, and below that a Leffel turbine wheel, with which he drove a pressure blower for his smelter, a flour mill and a two-stamp mill and concentrating table for treating the ore from the mines. After that the stream, having cooled, irrigated a forty-acre farm down below the hacienda.

Going out on the train I had told the conductor that when I came back I wanted to sample some piles of ore, about four hundred tons, which lay on the ground at a siding, and he said he would stop the train and hold it while I took the samples. When I came back the manager of the road was aboard, and I was afraid the conductor might not stop with him along; so I asked the conductor about it, and he said "Who the hell do you suppose is running this road? Of course I'll stop for you." When he stopped, the manager got off with me, and held the sacks while I took the samples, which took about half-an-hour. I thought, "Where could such a thing as this happen except in Mexico?"[5]

This local manager in Chihuahua was, I think, the most handsome man I have ever seen, about six feet tall, perfect physique, oval face with smooth olive complexion, wide lustrous brown eyes, always immaculately dressed. He was also the only person to whom I ever refused credit. He had two mines, one at Santa Eulalia and one at Cusihuiriachi, from which he shipped ore to the Chihuahua smelter, and brought me the smelter samples to assay, but he showed no disposition to pay my bill. One day, when his *mozo* came for his assay certificate, I told him he would have to bring the money to pay for it before I gave it to him, and that was the regular procedure thereafter. I was much annoyed when I first went there by the ubiquitous bill collectors. It was the custom, instead of sending bills out by mail, to send by a collector, who would wait for payment, unless he was told to return at a set time later. They always seemed to come just at my busiest time of day, when I did not have time to stop and write a check. I found that it seemed to be a habit with most

Mexicans, as well as some other nationals, not to pay an obligation until forced to do so. It was no uncommon sight to see a collector dressed in red, standing before a door, and every while rapping on it with a cudgel and asking payment of a bill, until the debtor finally succumbed.

Another thing that annoyed me was the seeming disposition of many Mexicans to disregard promises. One day I mentioned a case in which one of the most prominent men in town had made me a promise and reiterated it, to lease me a house he owned when the lease to the incumbent expired, but leased it to someone else, to an attorney, and he said, "That man had made you no promise, and would be astonished and indignant, if you accused him of breaking a promise. In Mexico no promise is made unless it is recorded in the book of a notary, signed by both parties and witnesses, and the stamps required by law affixed and cancelled by them. That is not only the law, but a fact which you should bear in mind." I found that Mexicans seemed to recognize it as peculiarity of Americans that they regarded their oral, or merely written, word as binding.

When I went to Chihuahua there were no automobiles there yet, and one of my customers said that it was his ambition to own the first one there, but he failed to achieve it. A local hardware firm took the agency for REO cars, and soon the red REO cars were running about the streets, but he did not own one.[6] I made mine examinations, which helped my income some, and I bought gold and silver bullion, which also helped, as there was a constant influx of bullion from small producers in the mountains.

One day a Mexican phoned me that he was sending me a man who, he believed, had found the lost Tayopa Mine, one of the most famous of the many mines lost when the Indians revolted against the Spanish padres, and drove them out of northern Mexico and New Mexico.[7] One of those mines is a gold mine in Mt. Franklin, within the city limits of El Paso, which has been rediscovered and cleaned out. Many people had searched for the Tayopa Mine, and one of them, an American whom I knew, had an apparently authentic document, made by the padre in charge of the mine, telling of the abandonment of the mine, with a map showing its location, which he had found in the archives of the cathedral at Seville, Spain.

Not long before this I had been to Guaynopa, to examine the Guaynopa, another "lost" mine, which was supposed to be in the same region as the Tayopa, and which had been recently rediscovered and acquired by two American mining engineers who were working it and wished to sell it to my clients. The two Mormon guides who had taken me to the Guaynopa Mine, went down by there the next day, starting out on an expedition to find the Tayopa Mine.[8] Several years later I met one of them in El Paso, and he said they had to give up their expedition, because they could not find a landing place in the vertical wall of the cañon of the Aros River for the raft with which they ferried it. The man with the bullion and two companions, all evident "*campesinos*," came, and after making sure that there was no one but me about, unrolled a piece of bullion from his *zarape*, which I saw at once was the small end of a cone-shaped ingot of silver, typical of those made by the old padres, but no longer in vogue, which showed that it had been buried a long time.[9] The ingot, of which it was a piece, was much larger than any I had seen. They never took their eyes off me while I weighed and sampled and assayed it, and went away without saying a word when I paid them. But the next morning they came with the central section of the ingot, and the third morning with the rest of it, and a couple of pounds of sawdust from sawing it up. The whole ingot weighed about seventy-five pounds, and I paid them what must have seemed a fortune.[10]

Then the spokesman, José de la Luz Lucero, told me they had found an old tunnel when they were out hunting in the rugged country south of the Aros River. They had spied the mouth of the tunnel high up in the steep ridge south of the river, and had been two days getting up to it, suffering with thirst, for though they could see the river all the time, they could not get down to it. Finally they struck a ledge, along which they walked to the mouth of the tunnel. The tunnel had had an iron door, which was according to tradition, but it had rusted away, and they found the bullion buried inside. When he left he said he had more bullion, and would bring it after the rainy season was over in October or November, so he could cross the Aros River. I never saw him again, and I thought that he probably was prevented from coming by the revolution, which began in November, and made communication with the Sierra Madres difficult. A mining engineer friend of mine who had a commission to try to find the Tayopa Mine got his address from me, and said that he found him, but could get no information from him, which is not surprising, whether his story was true or not.

In the Guaynopa Mine the methods used by the Spaniards in mining in hard rock were clearly shown. They would drill a row of holes about three inches in diameter along the wall of the ore, half [of] the hole in the wall, half in the ore. Then they filled the hole almost full of quicklime, poured in some water, and drove a tight wooden plug into the end of the hole. The swelling lime cracked the rock, so they could pick it out. There was plenty of limestone at hand, so they burned their own lime right there, and this was a cheap method, where explosives were scarce and expensive. At the Guaynopa Mine the vein outcropped in the vertical wall of a cañon, and a big bunch of high-grade silver ore stuck right out into the cañon, so they started a tunnel into the wall, taking out ore as they went in. When they were driven away, they bulkheaded the entrance, and covered it with rocks and gravel, and the stream no doubt soon washed down debris and covered all trace of it. Then after a long time the stream went on a tear, and washed away the covering so the entrance was exposed again.

One day a man who was teaching English in the Institute, which corresponds to our high school, came and begged me to substitute for him while he took a vacation, someone who had promised to substitute having failed at the last minute. The recitations were from 7 to 8 a.m., so they would not interfere with my business, so I finally reluctantly consented. He never came back, so I stayed on. As there was no heat in the schools, they sometimes suffered with the cold in winter, and the yearly vacation, which was for only one month, was for the month of December. At the beginning of the year the director notified me that my recitation period had been changed to 11 a.m. to noon, and when I told him I could not come at that hour, he told me I must find someone to take my place, as the law forbade me to quit without permission from the governor, and he (the director) would not recommend such permission until I found a suitable teacher. I finally induced the athletic director of the Y.M.C.A., an Australian, to take the job. In the years afterward I sometimes had reason to be glad of the acquaintances I had made among these high school boys, after they grew up.

There was no corporeal punishment in the schools, and at the Institute the instructors had nothing with enforcing discipline, except to warn offenders, and after recitations, to write in a book kept for that purpose in the director's office, stating the punishment to be meted out. For the boys this was attended to by the "*velador*," a big handsome young fellow, and for the girls by the "*veladora*," a handsome middle-aged lady, both with beautiful manners, but firm as to discipline. One of the usual modes of discipline was to put the pupil under arrest, sometimes for as long as six days, holding him there at the school, where there was ample room, it having once been a convent, with buildings and courtyards which covered two city blocks.

As a text-book I had to use one written by an Englishman, with such spellings as "labour," and such terms as "tram" and "lift" for street-car and elevator, and many modes of expression differing from the American style. I tried to explain these differences to my pupils, but I fear with little success. I was instructed not to talk to them in Spanish, which was no doubt a wise provision, as my Spanish was very bad. I found that I could learn Spanish faster than any other way by reading the daily newspapers, an idea I got from the memoirs of Carl Schurz, who learned English that way.[11] Mining terms I soon acquired by reading mine reports in Spanish.

Rent houses have always been scarce in Chihuahua, and it was six months after I went there before I could get a house that I was satisfied to live in, and then I had to buy the furniture of the tenant who was vacating, before he would turn his lease over to me. The building was on a street corner, and the very corner was occupied by a little Mexican grocery, the owner of which had four children about the same ages as my four; so they played together, and it seemed no time at all until all my children were talking Spanish better than I speak it today, and it was not very long before I noticed that the two younger ones habitually spoke Spanish when they were playing together.[12]

In 1910, the centennial year of Mexican independence, President Díaz was scheduled to pay Chihuahua a visit, and because of his interest in the growth of the schools it was decided to present him with an album containing the pictures of all the schools and school authorities and teachers in Chihuahua; so I was instructed to have my photograph taken at the expense of the state. I think it was the best picture I have ever had made. So my picture is filed in the Mexican archives, but not in the rogues' gallery.

When we had been there three years we decided that it would be best to send all our children to the United States to school, so my wife went with them to Valparaiso, Indiana, and rented a house and looked after them during the school term, returning to Chihuahua for the summer vacation.[13]

Among my customers was the local agent of the National Railways, whose uncle and another man had a silver mine in the sierra west of Chihuahua. When I told him what I would charge him for looking after his shipments to the sampling works, he said that the partner who was working the mine carefully estimated the value of each carload before shipping it, and he said he would pay me, in addition to my regular charges, one peso per carload for each ounce of silver per ton I could [produce] from the buyer in excess of that estimate, to which I of course assented. The ore kept getting better with every carload, and pretty soon there was a carload on which I got a bonus of fifty pesos. The owners of this mine were very anxious to sell it, as they thought they had only a chimney of ore, and were afraid to drift away from the shaft, for fear that they would run out of ore, and afraid to sink the shaft deeper, for fear that the water would drown them out. Many engineers had looked at the mine, and turned it down at a very moderate price. Finally they sold it to a prominent citizen of Chicago for $100,000, plus a commission of $10,000 to the man who made the sale, and they were delighted. Afterward they came into my office and loudly bewailed having sold the mine too cheaply. The buyer is generally believed to have made a clear profit of at least $15,000,000, all this rich ore coming from a piece of ground containing only five or six acres.

One day in the summer of 1910 my Mexican helper said suddenly, "There is going to be a revolution." I said, "When?" He said, "November 20." I asked him how he knew, but he would only say, "I know." None of us foreigners thought there would be any more revolutions, at least not during the rule of Porfirio Díaz, so I just laughed, and thought no more about it. But on November 20 the revolution commenced, the beginning of the decline of Mexico, which is still going on.[14]

It was started as a local revolt against certain taxes and against the political clique in power in the Chihuahua State Government, and the revolters numbered not more than three hundred, mostly small farmers and cattle men, and at first they made no effort to take possession of the City of Chihuahua, but started the revolt as a riot in the town of Guerrero, in the mountains a hundred miles or so west of Chihuahua. When a trainload of state troops was sent out to quell the riot, it was ambushed about halfway out, the troops were driven from the train, the commander killed, and the troops vanished. We foreigners all thought Don Porfirio would promptly send a big force of federal troops, and quickly quell the revolt; but Don Porfirio delayed, and finally sent General Navarro with only six hundred men. He started out afoot to the rescue of the state troops, who were supposed to be encamped about seventy-five miles west of Chihuahua, but encountered the rebels a little way out of town, and fought a battle which resulted in the retreat of the rebels, and the return of the federal troops to town to await reinforcements. I saw this battle through a telescope from the bell-tower of a church in town, and I have some snapshots taken in the field by the correspondent of the *Mexican Herald* who accompanied General Navarro, one of which shows the only casualty suffered by the federals: the General's horse holding up his foot, which had just been struck by a bullet. They brought in two prisoners, and marched them down the middle of the street past my office to the jail, but they turned out to be the burro milk men on their way to town to deliver milk.[15]

Then Francisco I. Madero came from down south and took charge of the revolt, and made a national affair of it. He had been the defeated candidate against Díaz in the last election, had been imprisoned for a while by Díaz, and had instigated a revolt against Díaz in Pachuca, which had been put down in a few hours. He made his headquarters at the great Bustillo Ranch, one of whose owners was his uncle, and here a notorious bandit, Doroteo Arango, who had assumed the name of Francisco Villa, offered to join him with four hundred men, mounted and fully equipped.[16]

The other revolt leaders were opposed to the admission of Villa, some of them having been victims of his raids, but Madero overruled them, saying that he could not afford to turn down such an offer. Pascual Orozco, who was one of the original plotters of the revolt, and had headed it until Madero came, was never on friendly terms with Villa. The reinforcements from Mexico City finally arrived, and set out for Bustillo's, but Madero's forces had already left there, going toward Ciudad Juárez, the town across the Rio Grande River from El Paso. The federal troops caught up with them, and they had some fights, but nothing decisive until they reached Juárez, which they besieged and took by assault after a few days, probably on account of the impatience of a lot of American soldiers of fortune with Madero, who started an attack without orders.[17]

When Díaz heard of the capture of Juárez, he resigned and left the country for Spain, and after some time died in Paris. Madero and his army made a triumphal entry into Chihuahua without firing a shot, and later into Mexico City. During the triumphal entry my helper said that Pancho Villa was outside, and there he was: a plump, very dark, round-faced man, with black curly hair almost like a Negro's, on a big black horse in front of the barber shop next door. Everyone was hopeful that, the revolution over, with no fighting in Chihuahua and almost no damage, life might resume its former prosperous course. But the revolutionary spirit had got possession of the people, and the former rulers of the State of Chihuahua, the so-called "científicos," were anxious to get back into control.[18] Madero and his advisers were not very capable rulers, and were rapidly dissipating the surplus Díaz had left in the treasury.[19]

Everywhere the revolutionists were showing their lack of ability and experience in the administration of the government. Pascual Orozco, who had wanted to be appointed Governor of Chihuahua, but had instead been made commander of the "Rurales," the federal mounted police, was much dissatisfied. So the "Científicos" got hold of him, and persuaded him that Madero had betrayed him and the country, and that it was up to him, as an organizer of the revolution, to save the country, and gave him fifty thousand pesos to start a revolution against Madero.

Shortly before this [Antonio] Rojas, who had been a colonel in the Madero army, got drunk and raised a disturbance in Dolores, a mining town in the Sierra Madre, and with a little group of men marched out of town, saying that he was going to start a revolution. The rurales arrested him, and brought him in to the penitentiary, which was near my house. A few mornings later we were awakened by a terrific crackling and banging, which I thought was from firecrackers and firing of guns in celebration of one of the new revolutionary holidays. The barracks of the state troops [were] just back of my house, between it and the penitentiary, and the revolutionary soldiers were addicted to firing their guns on almost any pretext.[20]

After breakfast I started to walk downtown as usual, along a wood yard which occupied all the rest of the block in which my house was the only one, at the upper end, and stretching across to the barracks, which was next to the penitentiary, and on the other side of the street the high wall of a schoolhouse which occupied the block. Then I noticed rurales down the street, beckoning and shouting to me to hurry, and discovered that I was in the midst of fusillade between a lot of men behind the schoolhouse wall, shooting at the penitentiary and the barracks, and the guards and soldiers and rurales defending them. The bullets were coming thick over my head, and I learned there the difference in the sounds of a Mauser bullet, which makes a little sharp whisper, and a 30–30, which makes a clattering racket. I was badly scared, but afraid to run, for fear they would start shooting at me, if they saw me running.

When I got to the rurales sheltered by the corner building, they explained that a crowd of two or three hundred men had come in from Dolores in the night, and attacked the penitentiary, demanding that Rojas be freed. The "battle" kept up another hour or two, when the attackers' ammunition was exhausted, and they retired, but the guards at the penitentiary held up the warden, and demanded that he let Rojas out on parole, to go and see the governor and to come back, if the governor refused to liberate him.

The warden let him go, and I met him going down to the State House as I went home to lunch, and again as I went down town after lunch, returning from the State House, where the governor had refused to release him. This time he was marching up the middle of the street with a little rabble of boys and old men. Just after I met him he stopped at a house on the corner where he should [have] turned off to go to the penitentiary, where a girl lived that he was courting, and came out with a rifle, and brandished it and shouted, "Who will go with Rojas and start a revolution," and they all, not more than twenty, all unarmed but Rojas, and mostly boys and old men, shouted "¡Viva Rojas!" Instead of going back to the penitentiary, they went on out past my house to the outskirts of town and camped there, and sent word to the governor that he had started a revolution, and that, if he did not send him within four hours at least four hundred pesos worth of food and supplies, he would attack the State House. The governor sent him what he demanded, and the next morning, his army considerably increased by volunteers, he set forth along the line of the Mexico Northwestern Railroad on a recruiting and foraging expedition for his revolution. Thus easily were revolutions started in those days.

A few days later Orozco, who had some three thousand well-equipped rurales in Chihuahua, started his revolution, using the rurales as a nucleus for his army and taking in Rojas and his band. The governor went into hiding, and Orozco took possession of the state government, and sent an army south to meet the army Madero was sending to suppress the revolt.[21] Orozco routed them in southern Chihuahua, and their remnants straggled into Torreón a disorganized rabble, and the general in command, who was also the Secretary of War, suicided. Orozco, instead of following up his advantage, remained where he was, giving Madero time to assemble a new army under General Huerta, who made a leisurely expedition and defeated Orozco, who retreated north and entrenched himself anew in steep and narrow Bachimba Pass, about a hundred miles south of Chihuahua.[22]

When this revolution started all Americans had been warned by the State Department that they could not be protected by their government, and were advised to leave Mexico until the revolution should be over; so most of us had sent out our families but remained ourselves. As my house was in an exposed situation, near the outskirts of town, I sent my family to El Paso, installed an old Mexican and his wife as caretakers, and went down town to live with the manager of the telephone company, who had sent his family out and had a big house right in the center of town, taking my Chinaman cook with me. An American groceryman came also to live with us, and with three others who came in for their meals we formed a mess, with my Chinaman for cook and the grocer as commissary.[23]

After Orozco had been defeated, it was rumored that he said that, if he should be defeated again in his new location, he would come back to Chihuahua and kill every American there. So the American consul called a meeting at his office, and we made arrangements to have a special train waiting inside the high-walled yard of the railroad shops, and a system for notifying everyone quickly if danger seemed imminent. We brought what firearms and ammunition we had and left them at the consulate for general use. Most all Mexicans hate Americans, but I have had some very good friends among them.[24]

At this time I met the federal assayer on the street, and he said, "I hear that Orozco has threatened to kill all the Americans if he is defeated. If he is, come right to my house with your family, and I will take care of you." Orozco was defeated and his army came straggling back into Chihuahua by ones and twos and little groups, but Huerta did not pursue at once, so he had time to loot the big stores and warehouses, and to load six long trains with all kinds of supplies, and then he went north to Villa Ahumada, with about three thousand men. He took a wrecking train with him, and destroyed the railroad behind him for seventy-five miles, burning the ties, heating rails on the burning ties, and twisting them around telegraph poles, as they could not be used, burning the wooden bridges and culverts and station houses and water tanks, and blowing up the stone and steel ones, and even burning the telegraph poles. It took five thousand men six months to restore that line so that a train could run on it.[25]

On July 4th, 1912, General Huerta took possession of Chihuahua, and the Americans, who had planned a Fourth of July banquet that evening at the Hotel Palacio, turned it into a banquet for Huerta and his staff. By chance, I got a seat across the narrow table from him. After the banquet we adjourned to the Foreign Club, Huerta taking one of his regimental bands, which had been playing at the banquet, to play there. As the bandsmen entered, one of them caught sight of a full-length portrait of Porfirio Díaz in the reading room. Off went his cap, and he made a profound bow and called the attention of the others to the picture, and all went through the same performance.[26]

Huerta had his headquarters in Chihuahua for several months, pursuing his campaign against Orozco, who had possession of the State of Chihuahua except the larger towns and the Mexico Northwestern Railroad. Huerta was friendly to Americans, and was made an honorary life member of the Foreign Club, where he spent a large part of his time, drinking in the patio. After Orozco left, the governor emerged from hiding, but Huerta was the real governor.

After the Madero revolution, Pancho Villa had been rewarded by Madero with a large gift of money, and had bought a ranch out in the sierra west of Chihuahua, and settled down to a ranchero's life. When the Governor had first got wind of Orozco's pending revolt, he had sent word to Villa to assemble his men and come in to help him, but he was too late. Villa later took his force, about six hundred men, to meet Huerta as he came from Mexico City, and joined his army. Villa had a fine horse, and Huerta sent to take possession of it for his own use, but Villa refused to give it up, and in the quarrel slapped Huerta's face, for which Huerta had him court-martialed and sentenced to be shot; but two of Madero's brothers who were with Huerta pleaded for him, and persuaded Huerta to send him to Mexico City for trial.[27] He was kept in the penitentiary there for six months or so, where he learned to read and write a little, at least enough to sign his name. He then escaped and made his way around through the U.S. to his home.

I had to make a trip to Arizona that summer, so I took a train on the Mexico Northwestern to go to Juárez, scheduled as a twelve-hour trip, but I was six days making it, partly owing to floods and landslides, and partly owing to Orozco's men having burned twenty-two bridges along the line. The superintendent of bridge construction furnished two handcars and men to work them for the nine Americans on the train, and we traveled about thirty-five miles that way, all hands carrying the hand-cars across the streams or ravines where the bridges were gone. Then we rode in the caboose of a work train into Juárez. Not long after that the "Red Flaggers," as Orozco's men were called, stopped a freight train at a tunnel, set it afire and sent it into the tunnel. Soon a passenger train came along, and, the signal showing all clear, went into the tunnel and was burned up. No one escaped. There were eleven Americans aboard, including the superintendent and express manager, a new man and a friend of mine, who, only a few days before, had been telling me why he gave up a job he had for that one. This guerrilla warfare continued for some time, without apparent advantage to either side.[28]

After a while Huerta was recalled to Mexico City, leaving General Rábago in charge. Pretty soon Félix Díaz, a nephew of Porfirio and a general in the federal army, started a revolution in Mexico City against the Madero regime. General Huerta, in charge of the defenses, joined Díaz after a few days, and had Madero and the Vice-President Pino Suárez murdered, and had himself made provisional president, and later elected president.

As soon as Madero was deposed, Orozco came into Chihuahua and declared fealty to the Huerta regime, saying that the object of his revolution had been realized in the deposition of Madero, and his army was incorporated into the federal army, in which he was made a general. Our hopes for peace and a chance to go about our business were soon blasted, as Pancho Villa and Venustiano Carranza, a friend of Madero, started revolutions against Huerta, and joined forces. Chihuahua was soon in a state of virtual siege again, with more soldiers in town than there had ever been, and so many military bands that we had concerts in two of the plazas every afternoon and evening, and we were awakened every morning at 5:30 by a band playing in the bandstand in the big park directly across the street from my house.

My family had come back when Orozco desisted and peace seemed likely.[29] Villa had got some six-inch cannons, but did not seem to have much ammunition for them, as he did not shoot more than a hundred shells into town. One of them burst just over my house one forenoon, and the slugs and fragments rattled down onto the roof and into the patio where I was, but did no damage. Of course I dodged quickly into the doorway after the danger was past. There were numerous attacks, one lasting three days and nights, and the sound of machine guns and French 75mm field guns became familiar, but Villa seemed unable to carry the city. Then he sent secretly at night two or three hundred men to Terrazas, a railroad station about thirty miles north of Chihuahua, held up a trainload of coal bound for Chihuahua, unloaded the coal and loaded his men on and went to Juárez.[30] They arrived early in the morning before daylight, all being quiet, as they had seized the operator at Terrazas before he could give the alarm. They had their own operator wire that the train was returning to Juárez on account of danger of capture, and that they had seized operators as they went north. They kept Juárez advised of the train's progress, so it was expected, and this allowed them to run the train right on past the station into the center of town. They had possession before the federal soldiers found it out.

Several trainloads of troops set out from Chihuahua for Juárez at once, but Villa went out to meet them, and they were routed and went straggling back to Chihuahua, where consternation reigned. Orders came from Mexico City to evacuate [Chihuahua], and there was scurrying around to get ready. All the rollingstock of the Orient Railroad was commandeered, and long lines of freight cars loaded with all kinds of things, from hay to pianos. The State Palace and the Federal Building were vacated, the banks were closed and the money taken away, except six hundred thousand pesos in ten-peso gold pieces belonging to the Banco Minero, which was concealed by pouring it into a hollow iron column of the main banking room.[31]

Many people left by wagon and auto. My helper said he would have to go, as he belonged to the Guardia Civil, a volunteer institution to maintain order in the city whenever the constituted authority failed, and Villa would kill him when he found it out. I tried to get him to stay, and told him I would keep him hidden in an upper room over my office, and I did not think Villa would do anything to him for serving in the Guardia Civil, as he had never fought against Villa. But he was afraid, and went with the army, and was killed in the fighting at Ojinaga.[32] Don Luis Terrazas, reputed to be the richest man in Mexico, left for Ojinaga and El Paso in his mahogany and plate-glass Concord coach, drawn by ten perfectly matched white Spanish mules, which he used to make the circuit of his haciendas twice a year.

Two people who had to leave, and who had fine houses in my neighborhood, offered me their houses just as they were, with servants, water and electricity paid, if I would stay in them, to keep the Villistas from occupying them. The agent from whom I rented my house begged me not to leave, and said I should have it rent-free, if only I would stay. He had to leave. I lived on the Paseo Bolívar, a wide boulevard, directly across the street from the bandstand in the largest park in town, so we had plenty of music, especially in revolutionary times, when there were many military bands.

After a few days Villa made his unopposed triumphal entry, and as he passed down our street he paused frequently while his men notified most of the people living in our block that they must vacate at once, as the houses were needed. The house next to me on one side was the home of Don Luis Terrazas' general manager, and it was occupied at once by a colonel and his staff, who rode their horses through the front gate, up the stone steps and through the front door, and stabled them in the patio. Officers in the revolutionary armies from generals down were very seldom trained or experienced soldiers, but more likely to be peons who had always lived in hovels, and did not know how to live in a good house.

Most of the houses on our block were seized, and I soon received notice that I must see the administrator of confiscated property, and arrange to pay rent on my house to him. After some discussion, in which I insisted that I should not be made to pay rent, on account of my arrangement with the agent of the owner, and because the revolution had ruined my business, so that I could not afford to pay rent, he agreed to a rental of twenty pesos a month for a trial period of three months, by which time he thought business would be much improved, and he would then make me a formal lease, presumably at a higher rate. When the three months was up, I went to the cashier, and paid six months more at the twenty-peso rate, and continued to pay at that rate as long as the Villa regime lasted. Villa money in the meantime was depreciating to one cent per peso in U.S. money, so that I was paying twenty cents U.S. a month for rent and water. I had been paying the equivalent of thirty dollars U.S., besides the water, which was a very low rental.

Villa hated Spaniards, so as soon as he came in he ordered that all Spaniards should be deported within twenty-four hours, and their property seized. He had a special train made up for them, and herded them onto it, about three hundred, and went through the train himself, to see that all Spaniards were aboard, and jeered at them, and seemed in high spirits. A German veterinarian whom I knew had a Spanish wife, and she had to go, so he went, too. Most of the Spaniards were merchants, some of them quite wealthy, and these had to pay a heavy ransom to escape with their lives.

El Nuevo Mundo, the biggest mercantile concern in town—with a stock of general merchandise worth at least a million dollars, with a four-story stone building covering half a block, and with huge warehouses—belonged to Spaniards in Mexico City. Villa put in a manager, who sold off the stock at less than half its value. Villa soon started out after the retreating federal army, which had gone to Ojinaga, on the Rio Grande River opposite Presidio, Texas, and entrenched themselves there. The army forced civilians unable to maintain themselves across the river, to be taken to El Paso by U.S. authorities and interned in a stockade at Fort Bliss. Don Luis Terrazas leased Senator Fall's big house in El Paso and a lot of other houses, and supported some three hundred relatives and retainers, and many others settled down in El Paso until such times as they might be able to return to Chihuahua. Villa drove the federal army across the river, where they were disarmed by U.S. soldiers, and taken to Fort Bliss and interned in the stockade.[33]

When General Huerta was driven out of Mexico, he also came to Fort Bliss, and was interned in the hospital, where he died after a long illness, during which he hatched up another revolution. The chief general was to have been Pascual Orozco, who had been in hiding at Shafter, Texas, in an old mine, after he had escaped by swimming the river at the Battle of Ojinaga. They hoped to take advantage of the fighting between Villa and Carranza to take possession of all northern Mexico easily, Villa having taken practically his whole force to fight Carranza, and being in desperate straits. Villa began issuing paper money almost immediately, and declared all other money contraband, but allowed all who had other money to exchange it at par for his money for thirty days.

Notes

1. The governor of Chihuahua at the time of Worcester's arrival was Enrique Creel, "the country's leading banker, perhaps the most influential Mexican representative of foreign capital, and one of the nation's most important industrialists." Mark Wasserman, *Pesos and Politics: Business, Elites, Foreigners, and Government in Mexico, 1854–1940* (Stanford: Stanford University Press, 2015), 34.

2. Worcester's view of Chihuahua evokes a worldview shared by most, if not all, U.S. capitalists invested in Mexico during the Gilded Age. The state and nation were said to be "waking up," in Worcester's words, to the wider world of capitalist development. In strict materialist terms, Worcester's views were correct: new technological developments were being introduced into the region from American entrepreneurs. This view often took a problematic and nationalist turn, however, in marking Mexican and indigenous peoples as culturally inferior. For an in-depth examination of how the presence of railroads embodied this discourse, see Michael Matthews, *The Civilizing Machine: A Cultural History of Mexican Railroads, 1876–1910* (Lincoln: University of Nebraska Press, 2013).

3. The ambitions of the Kansas City, Mexico & Orient Railroad aligned with the lofty dreams of Albert K. Owen, founder of the socialist-capitalist utopian colony on Topolobampo Bay, one of the most fascinating histories in the borderlands. See Leopold Katscher, "Owen's Topolobampo Colony, Mexico," *American Journal of Sociology* 12, no. 2 (September 1906); José C. Valadés, "Topolobampo, La Metropoli Socialista de Occidente," *El Trimestre Económico* 6, no. 23 (October–December 1939); and Thomas A. Robertson, *A Southwestern Utopia* (Los Angeles: Ward Ritchie Press, 1947).

4. A trace of Don Demetrio Oaxaca appears in *The Mining World* of 1910, when Luis Terrazas Jr., acquired Oaxaca's interest in the Virgen Mine east of Chihuahua City. "Chihuahua," *The Mining World* 32, no. 13 (March 26, 1910), 682.

5. As with Worcester's previous comments on development in Mexico (see note 2), this question is laden with meaning and deeper cultural assumptions. One can sense incredulity in the question, remarking on the unregulated nature of Mexican industry and commerce, while also perhaps underscoring the power of foreign investors to have their way in foreign lands. It is a simple question that likely passed without second thought in Worcester's mind, but it does speak to an American mindset of capitalists working in a land perceived to be developmentally behind the United States.

6. "REO cars" were manufactured by Ransom Eli Olds, founder of the Olds Motor Works (later Oldsmobile and acquired by General Motors). In 1904 he incorporated the Reo Motor Car Company, "using Olds's initials after . . . Olds Motor Works had threatened to sue if the company employed the Olds name in its title." George S. May, "Olds, Ransom Eli," *American National Biography* (New York: Oxford University Press, 2000), https://doi.org/10.1093/anb/9780198606697.article.1001245. Last accessed January 28, 2020.

7. Legends of lost mines proliferated in borderland publications and by word of mouth. A common subset of these legends dealt with mines abandoned by the Spanish after 1816, with the independence of Mexico, and that American capital and ingenuity could reclaim these mines to make them productive again.

8. The Mormon guides were more than likely colonists in one of several settlements in Chihuahua, established there piecemeal after 1882 (passage of the Edmunds Act, which outlawed polygamy). Not all colonists relocated to Mexico purely for this reason. See, among other publications, Annie Richardson Johnson, *Heartbeats of Colonia Diaz* (Salt Lake City: Publishers Press, 1972); Nelle Spilsbury Hatch, *Colonia Juarez: An Intimate Account of a Mormon Village* (Salt Lake City: Deseret, 1954); and Thomas Cottam Romney, *The Mormon Colonies in Mexico* (Salt Lake City: Deseret, 1938).

9. "Campesino" is someone who lives or works in the countryside, and a "zarape" (or "serape," in contemporary orthography) is an often brightly colored, large shawl with fringes on the end, common to rural Mexico.

10. The timing of this anecdote is unclear. Assuming this transpired in January 1910, when silver averaged $0.53/ounce, the seventy-five-pound ingot would have fetched approximately $636, or, according the various estimates, between $12,800 and $17,700 in 2019 dollars. *Annual Report of the Director of the Mint for the Fiscal Year Ended June 30, 1911, and also Report on The Production of the Precious Metals in the Calendar Year 1910* (Washington DC: Government Printing Office, 1912), 319. Calculations made with MeasuringWorth.com, accessed January 29, 2020 (historical currency converter).

11. Carl Schurz was a German immigrant to the United States in 1852, and rose to fame as a newspaper editor, a U.S. Senator from Missouri, and later Secretary of the Interior under President Rutherford Hayes. On learning English, he wrote that his method "was very simple. I did not use an English grammar. I do not think I ever had one in my library. I resolutely began to read—first my daily newspaper, which happened to be the *Philadelphia Ledger*. Regularly every day I worked through editorial articles, the news letters and despatches, and even as many of the advertisements as my time

would allow." Carl Schurz, *The Reminiscences of Carl Schurz*, vol. 2, *1852–1863* (London: John Murray, 1909), 9–10.

12. This would have been Richard and Barbara, then approximately nine and six years old, respectively.

13. The Worcesters' daughter, Barbara, first attended school at the academy offered by the Congregational church in Chihuahua, founded by James and Gertrude Eaton. As American Protestant expatriates, they naturally shared a common bond and were close to the missionaries. For a history of the church, its school, and the reliance on gender to extend the Protestant mission, see Andrew Offenburger, *Frontiers in the Gilded Age: Adventure, Capitalism, and Dispossession from Southern Africa to the U.S.-Mexican Borderlands, 1880–1917* (New Haven: Yale University Press, 2019), chap. 3. According to Anne Rowe, "Barbara spoke Spanish fluently and used it professionally. She translated and taught Spanish to pay her way through Trinity University and then worked for Naval Intelligence during World War II and then worked for the American Red Cross up until her death in 1978 (age 78)." Correspondence with the author.

14. Worcester, a foreign businessman tied to American capital in Mexico, certainly understood the Revolution as a narrative of decline: that social upheaval harmed more than helped the nation. Plenty of historical incidents support this view, but one cannot discount jarring statistics on wealth inequality in the nation. On the cultural context of Porfirian Mexico, see, for example, William H. Beezley, *Judas at the Jockey Club and Other Episodes of Porfirian Mexico*, 2nd ed. (Lincoln: University of Nebraska Press, 2004). The historiography of the revolution is large, but the definitive account remains Alan Knight, *The Mexican Revolution*, 2 vols. (Cambridge: Cambridge University Press, 1986); see also his *U.S.-Mexican Relations, 1910–1940: An Interpretation* (San Diego: University of California at San Diego, Center for U.S.-Mexican Studies, 1987); John Mason Hart, *Revolutionary Mexico: The Coming and Process of the Mexican Revolution* (Berkeley: University of California Press, 1987), and, for an argument implicating American capital in the revolution, his *Empire and Revolution: The Americans in Mexico since the Civil War* (Berkeley: University of California Press, 2002). For succinct yet astute accounts of the longer revolution, see William H. Beezley and Colin M. MacLachlan, *Mexicans in Revolution, 1910–1946: An Introduction* (Lincoln: University of Nebraska Press, 2009); and Gilbert M. Joseph and Jürgen Buchenau, *Mexico's Once and Future Revolution: Social Upheaval and the Challenge of Rule since the Late Nineteenth Century* (Durham: Duke University Press, 2013).

15. Worcester is describing the government's early attempt to quash rebellious activity incited in part by Guerrero native Pascual Orozco Jr. in 1910. See Knight, *Mexican Revolution*, vol. 1, 176–81; and Mark Wasserman, "The Social Origins of the 1910 Revolution in Chihuahua," *Latin American Research Review* 15, no. 1 (1980).

16. Villa was born José Doroteo Arango Arámbula. For the definitive work on Villa, see Friedrich Katz, *The Life & Times of Pancho Villa* (Stanford: Stanford University Press, 1998).

17. Worcester is correct here. The attack on Ciudad Juárez began without Madero's orders, and its effect (in concert with other unrest in Mexico) was the abrupt downfall and exile of Porfirio Díaz.

18. The "científicos" were supporters of President Porfirio Díaz and typically came from well-connected classes in Mexico City or among the regional elite. Members of the Liberal Union who shared "a Comtian and 'scientific' view of society," these polit-

ical allies of Díaz prioritized "continued economic development: more railways, a rationalised fiscal system, the suppression of internal customs barriers, European immigration, and further cuts in the military budget." Knight, *Mexican Revolution*, vol. 1, 21.

19. Worcester has a jaundiced view of Madero, who could not deliver on his revolutionary aspirations nor lessen significantly the gap between rich and poor in Mexico. As the memoirist later recounts, two years after Madero's election, his political enemies organized a coup and coordinated his assassination, led by Victoriano Huerta and Díaz's nephew, Félix Díaz.

20. Worcester's chronology matches the historical record. He is referring to an incident with Antonio Rojas, a disaffected ex-Maderista who fought in Dolores and was "apprehended in Moris in January 1912, jailed in Chihuahua, and freed by a group of mounted rurales." *Diccionario Porrúa: Historia, Biografía y Geografía de México*, 5a Edición con un Suplemento (Mexico City: Editorial Porrúa, S.A., 1986 [1964]), 2501. More on Rojas: Francisco R. Almada, *La Revolucion en el Estado de Chihuahua, Tomo I* (Chihuahua: Talleres Gráficos de la Nación, 1964), 276–78.

21. With the outbreak of violence and factionalism, Knight suggests "Interim Governor Aurelio González was helpless." Knight, *Mexican Revolution*, vol. 1, 292.

22. This transpired in July 1912. "Mexican Guns Force Rebel Army Back; Orozco's Troops Retreat to North of Bachimba Pass from Federal Shells," *New York Times*, July 4, 1912, 5.

23. Worcester mentions "my Chinaman" in concert with contemporary parlance, but the brief reference evokes the broader, international borderland presence of Chinese immigrants. As in the American West, the Chinese had a pronounced presence in Mexico and the transnational region. See Robert Chao Romero, *The Chinese in Mexico, 1882–1940* (Tucson, University of Arizona Press, 2012). For a study situated after 1930, see Fredy González, *Paisanos Chinos: Transpacific Politics among Chinese Immigrants in Mexico* (Berkeley: University of California Press, 2017).

24. Worcester grossly overstates this, but there was significant anti-American sentiment, especially in Chihuahua and Sonora, leading up to and during the early Revolution. To suggest that "most all Mexicans hate Americans" reveals more about the mine manager's limited social circles and his later exposure to rough revolutionaries than it does about any widespread xenophobia.

25. This narrative coincides with the description in Miguel A. Sánchez Lamego, *Historia Militar de la Revolución Mexicana en la Epoca Maderista, Tomo III* (México: Instituto Nacional de Estudios Históricos de la Revolución Mexicana, 1977).

26. This anecdote lays bare the esteem that American investors held for Porfirio Díaz and the performative nature, almost ritualistic, of praising the former president.

27. Contemporary papers and national outlets like *Pearson's Magazine* did report that Villa had slapped Huerta's face, but historians' narrations of this encounter do not contain such a detail. Worcester likely confused this with another story involving Villa and William Benton. For a suspect telling, see Gerald Brandon, "Francisco Villa," *Pearson's Magazine* (July 1914), 76; for a more reliable telling, see Friedrich Katz, *The Life and Times of Pancho Villa* (Stanford: Stanford University Press, 1998), 164–65.

28. Worcester is likely recalling the "Cumbre Tunnel horror" of February 4, 1914, incorrectly attributed to Máximo Castillo in alliance with Orozco. "Bandits . . . set fire to the timber lining of the railroad tunnel by running a blazing freight train into it. A passenger train crashed into the burning freight train in the centre of the tunnel, and

not a single passenger escaped. Some of the bodies never were identified, but it was established that Mrs. Lee Carruth and her five small children, with ten other Americans, perished." *Current History: A Monthly Magazine of* The New York Times 11, no. 1 (January 1920), 38. The *New York Times* lists M. J. Gilmartin as Superintendent of the Mexican Northwestern Railroad at Chihuahua, and C. H. Marders as the express agent (whom, if correct, Worcester references in this manuscript). "Villa Tells Wilson He'll Punish Bandit," *New York Times,* February 9, 1914. Katz adds that after sending the passenger train in, bandits "blew up both exits of the tunnel, so that the passengers were either burned to death or suffocated," and he identifies the culprit, via Mexican historians, as Manuel Gutiérrez. Katz, *Pancho Villa,* 415.

29. This was in 1913.

30. The attack described here happened in mid-November 1913 and is discussed in Alan Knight, *The Mexican Revolution: Counter-revolution and Reconstruction,* vol. 2 (Lincoln: University of Nebraska Press, 1986), 115–16.

31. This transpired in November 1913 and is corroborated in Katz, *Pancho Villa,* 245. Katz, citing a bank report, writes the amount was $590,000.

32. Ojinaga fell on January 10, 1914.

33. The forces led "3,300 Huerta troops, 1,067 women, and 312 children from Presidio to the railroad in Marfa, from where they were transported to a prisoner of war stockade established at Fort Bliss. The camp was built on the mesa beyond the fort and was surrounded by barbed wire. The prisoners lived in tents." Charles H. Harris and Louis R. Sadler, *The Secret War in El Paso: Mexican Revolutionary Intrigue, 1906–1920* (Albuquerque: University of New Mexico Press, 2016), 157.

5

Business in the Borderlands, 1914–1939

THE MINING DISTRICT OF GUANACEVÍ, DURANGO, FOR A
year or so had had railroad connection cut off, so that ore could
not be shipped to the smelters, and money could not be obtained
to continue work. The principal mining operators issued scrip
to pay their employees and local bills, and kept on working, pil-
ing up the ore until such time as they might ship it, so there was
a lot of that scrip in circulation, which came into the treasury
in exchange for Villa money. When they could ship again, Villa
ordered the proceeds from the shipments to be paid into the
treasury until the scrip was all redeemed at thirty-five cents U.S.
per peso, the price at which he had pegged his currency. They
agreed that I should be "*interventor*" to carry out this decree,
this being in my line of business, which included attending to
shipments to smelters and making settlement for them.

In the spring of 1914, owing to difficulties between the U.S.
and Mexico, Americans were warned again that their government could not protect them or their property, and advised
them to leave the country at once. So I went to El Paso, and my
family went on to California for the summer, leaving my assistant to attend to what little business there might be, and a Mexican woman servant in the house.

Another man and I had bought a lot of copper tanks and fit-
tings of a soda water factory that had burned down, and had
intended to ship them to El Paso. One of Villa's men noticed
them and told me not to ship them, as they wanted the copper

to make copper money. He told me to see the colonel in charge of the Compañia Industrial, a big foundry and machine shop which Villa had seized, and he would buy it, which he did, and made one-, two-, five-, and ten-cent pieces out of it.

A German friend wired me to El Paso that he had to move, and asked me to let him use my house until he could find another, and I told him to move in, but to keep the servant and to keep a little bedroom reserved for me when I should come on my business trips. Soon I made a trip to exchange drafts for scrip at the treasury, just a few days after the World War started. As soon as he saw me, my German friend asked what I thought about the war, to which I replied that Germany was going to get a good licking, which she deserved. He replied, "Impossible! Germany is too great. The whole world couldn't whip Germany." He asked me if I thought the United States would come into it. I said yes, that whenever it looked like the British might be getting the worst of it, the U.S. would come to their rescue, as we could not afford to let Germany conquer Britain. He could not believe this either.

The great majority of Mexicans were favorable to Germany, the Germans and the German government for a long time having carried on active propaganda glorifying Germany and especially belittling America and Americans. In every important city in Mexico, the German government maintained a school, which was always the best in town, and it was a center of propaganda for Germany and against the United States, as was also the office of the German consul. At the time of the American occupation of Vera Cruz, there was a mass meeting at the state theatre, at which the German consul made a speech in which he declared that all Mexico's ills were due to America and Americans.[1] This is the attitude of most Mexicans toward the U.S. and its citizens.

In the fall of 1914 things began to look better, and business began to pick up some, so we went back to Chihuahua. I was having trouble with my bullion buying. The railroad and express was in the hands of the Villa government, and shipment of bullion out of the country was prohibited, so I had to stop buying. I already had quite a [bit] on hand in the bank vault, which I could not send out. A friendly Mexican engineer, who was high in the Villa councils, told me that Villa was about to commence coining silver money. I asked him to get permission from Villa for me to ship out my bullion so I could go on with my buying unmolested, offering all silver bullion I might buy first to the treasury at two cents an ounce less than the current New York price, and if they did not want it, I should be allowed to ship it wherever I pleased. Villa told him to tell me to come and see him, which I did, and told him what I wanted, and he said he would write me a letter agreeing to my proposition; but he was very busy entertaining General Obregon, who had come from Mexico City as an envoy from Carranza, with whom Villa was having some disputes, so I must come back in a week, when the letter would be ready for me.

A day or two after he had his final quarrel with Carranza, and when I went to see him again, he said he had been too busy—getting his army ready to start for Mexico City to fight Carranza—to think about any private matters, so I would have to wait. He left in a day or two, and did not return for many months, and I do not think I ever saw him again. My bullion stayed in the bank vault, and Villa did not mint any silver coins for a long time. Finally, he coined about one hundred thousand silver pesos late in 1915. Soon after, he was driven out of Chihuahua by Carranza, and that money was declared contraband, so most of it was melted down. I bought five hundred or more of them, and I still have three.

We had several different kinds of money in circulation during revolutionary times, all of which are now obsolete. In the mining town of Urique the people refused to accept the Villa currency, and as all other money had been declared contraband, there was no money. So a doctor from Rochester, N.Y., who had a silver mine there, melted some of his bullion into slugs of all sizes, from three cents to more than three pesos, and stamped the value on them with ordinary numbering dies. He paid his men and his local bills with them, the only money in vogue there for some time. I have some of it now, which I bought from him with other bullion.

Chihuahua was the center of a great mining region. It was also a smelting center, and there are said to have been as many as three hundred Castilian smelting and refining furnaces along the Chuviscar River, which runs through the city. Much of the city is built on the great slag piles from these furnaces, and the streets are macadamized with it. Much of this slag still contained enough silver and lead to make it worthwhile to smelt it over again at the big modern smelter there, so I bought some of it and shipped it to the smelter for a year or two during the Villa regime. When the Huerta forces evacuated Chihuahua, the banks all closed, and Villa took possession of them when he came in.

He somehow got wind of the concealment of gold by the Banco Minero, and he had Luis Terrazas Jr., Vice President of the bank, who had rashly stayed in the city, arrested and taken at night to a grove at the edge of town and hanged three times, until he was unconscious and apparently dead, but was finally revived and disclosed the hiding place of the gold.[2]

Soon after this Villa bought a ranch in the outskirts of town from a German-American friend of mine, and paid him forty thousand pesos, all in ten-peso gold pieces. Villa had the hacienda rebuilt in grand style, and lived there part of the time. He seized a fine house on the Paseo Bolívar belonging to one of the Terrazas family, where he lived part of the time with one of his wives, and another fine house for his office. Later he built a forty-room house in town, but I think it was never quite completed. His widow lives there now, and carries on some kind of charitable institution there.[3] He also built an ornate red granite mausoleum for himself in a cemetery in town. Villa confiscated a lot of mines and mills, and a smelter at Santa Rosalía, about a hundred miles south of Chihuahua, which was used to smelt the ore from the confiscated mines, with an American metallurgist in charge.

One of the mines in southern Chihuahua had a big body of good zinc ore, and he made a contract to ship twenty thousand [tons] of it to a zinc smelter in St. Louis. I was to look after the smelter's interests in Chihuahua, the contract requiring them to pay 75 percent of the estimated value of the ore before it should leave Chihuahua. The first shipment of five cars went through all right. The federal assayer and I each sampled and assayed it. I paid the export duties, the state tax, and the 75 percent of the estimated value to Villa's manager, and sent the lot on. The second lot of fifteen cars failed to stop at Chihuahua, but went right on to Juárez. As soon as they found it out, the zinc smelting company had its customs agent at Juárez pay the export duties there, and send the cars right on over the river, drew the money from the bank, which it had deposited to my account to pay on the ore and expenses in Chihuahua, and notified me that it would not pay for the ore. As soon as I found out what was going on, I notified Villa's manager, and he took the first train for Juárez; but he got there too late, as the ore had already gone.

I protested by wire and letter, and insisted that the smelter keep its contract, telling them that I would be held responsible, as their agent, and it would mean a very serious situation for me, but they ignored me. So the manager had me arrested, charged with conspiring with the zinc company to steal the ore. He explained to me privately at my preliminary hearing that he was very sorry to have to prosecute me, but he said, "You know Villa. If I don't produce this money he will kill me, and I have a wife and five children, so I must do the best I can to get the money. He won't kill you, for you are an American, and he wants the good will of Americans just now, so he will only hold you until the money is paid. I can't get hold of the smelting company, and you are the only one I can get hold of."

After a private preliminary hearing before the Villa "judge," a boy about twenty years old, not a lawyer, who got his instructions from Villa's Minister of Justice, he had me confined in the state penitentiary, pending formal trial.[4] Mexican law provides that persons who are committed to jail pending trial are to be kept "*incommunicado*" for seventy-two hours; but I was allowed to notify my wife and the American Consul and my assistant, and I was kept in a cell only one night, when I was transferred to the chapel, a big room on the second floor, with a big gothic French window opening on the main patio.

When Villa came into Chihuahua he had killed the priest, against whom he had some grudge. There was a lavatory and toilet, with running water, and an electric light which had lost its socket, but my friend the manager of the telephone company had that fixed for me right away. There was a double desk also, exactly like the one I had used in school in Greensburg. There was no bed, but I had a cot sent up from the office that I used in trips out in the country, and bed clothes from the house, and an oil stove, as it was winter, and there was no heat about the place except in the kitchen and the hospital.

The penitentiary was a modern stone building, built after I went to Chihuahua by U.S. contractors of stone, steel, and concrete, with cells of reinforced concrete and solid steel doors. Prisoners had to furnish their own bedclothes. Twice a week the prisoners took everything movable out of the cells, and they were flushed out with a hose. Every fifteen minutes through the night the guards in the towers on the wall, as well as all the city policemen, blew a little clay flageolet which makes several tones, and [cried] in a high-pitched wail, "A-l-e-r-t-a."

I was treated with great consideration. My door was never locked, so I was free to go about in the prison as I pleased, and I roamed about the place at my own sweet will, except into the cell corridors, which were kept locked. My wife or my daughter brought me my meals, as I did not care for the prison fare, although it was sufficient and nourishing, and no doubt as good as, perhaps better than, what most of the prisoners were used to at home. The bulls that were killed every Sunday at the Plaza de Toros were made into a stew with vegetables in it, and this furnished most of the meat of the diet, served only at the mid-day meal. At all meals they had black coffee, big crusty French

Business in the Borderlands

rolls or tortillas, and hot frijoles. No Mexican meal is complete without these latter, served at the end of the meal, usually in the little red earthen bowls in which they were cooked, just out of the oven or off the fire. They had chili regularly, which is also indispensable. There was no sugar, milk, butter, eggs, nor sweets.

I was allowed to have visitors at any time, and the next day after they put me in the chapel Don Luis Terrazas [Jr.] dropped in to see me, saying, "I see you are occupying my former quarters." After he had been hanged [nearly to death], they confined him in the penitentiary chapel for nine months. They had released him under the constant surveillance of two men just a few days before my arrest. He had had the old school desk put in there. One of his sons was in the penitentiary hospital, and he came to see him twice a week, and also dropped in to see me while I was there. After I was gone he was arrested and confined there again, and his son was kept there, and after a year or so he managed to bribe somebody, and he and his son escaped and got out to the U.S. by auto.

Across the hall from me was a big room, occupied by forty or fifty political and military prisoners. Directly underneath me on the ground floor, in a room the same size as mine, was confined General Rábago, Military Commander of the Northern Zone and Governor of the State of Chihuahua during the Huerta regime, with three other political prisoners. They had to do their own sweeping and cleaning up, which I suppose was to humiliate them, but trusties came twice a week and scrubbed my place, and swept it every other day. General Rábago was awaiting trial on the charge of murdering [Abraham] González, one of the three plotters of the Madero revolution, and the first revolutionary governor of Chihuahua.[5] His chances of survival were very slim, and he consumed a lot of brandy, which one day carried him off suddenly, before he was called for trial.

I had some influential friends in the U.S., and through them I managed to raise quite a hullabaloo about my arrest.[6] The U.S. consul, who was my near neighbor and good friend, and was not afraid of Villa, made a big fuss about it to the Villa authorities and demanded my release, and stirred up the State Department of the U.S. and the zinc company.[7] The Minister of Justice promised him to have me released on bail within twenty four hours, and I had two friends who qualified as bondsmen in the amount of $100,000; but later he said that the offense with which I was charged was unbailable, as it involved a sum greater than five hundred pesos. The State Department sent a special investigator, who did not see me nor the U.S. Consul, nor communicated with either of us. He went to see Villa's Minister of Justice, who told him that I was undoubtedly guilty, which he so reported to the State Department, controverting the very detailed statement of the consul that it was merely an attempt to extort money from me. I wrote Mr. Bryan, who was then Secretary of State, a statement of my case, and received a personal reply from him, detailing the effort he was making in my behalf, and promising to spare no effort to secure my liberty.[8]

After I had been there a few days, I told the assistant director that I did not want to take the cold shower baths, which were the only ones available to prisoners, and he said that he would let me go home that night, when he would be in charge, to take a bath. This deputy warden was a prisoner himself, a very nice fellow. He had been a rich wholesale merchant whose property Villa had confiscated, putting him in the penitentiary. In the evening, after the warden had gone home, a trusty came for me, and we went out by a little door from the penal court room. The trusty lived a block or two below the prison, and he stopped to see his family a little, while I waited outside, and then we went on to my house. He went in and waited while I took a bath and had an hour's visit with my family. The next time he stayed at home while I went for my visit, and we continued that procedure during the rest of my stay at the penitentiary.

I got acquainted with a number of the political and military prisoners. One of these was a handsome young fellow whose father was an Englishman and his mother a Mexican. He was a Villa army paymaster, and was in for misappropriation of funds. He was very friendly, and adopted me as his foster father. Another

Business in the Borderlands

of my friends was a Carranza major and newspaperman, a prisoner of war who had a typewriter and wrote daily editorials for a Chihuahua newspaper.

My friends brought me lots of things to read, among them some novels in Spanish. I had a folding camp chair sent up, and I spent a good deal of time sitting in the patio in the sun and improving my knowledge of Spanish. I read through *Jane Eyre* in Spanish.

There was only one other American confined there while I was there, a man who had gone from El Paso with a large sum of Carranza money to pay for a hotel he had bought in Victoria, capital of Tamaulipas, where only that kind of money was valid at that time. He got as far as Torreón, where he was arrested by the Villa police. His money was taken away, and he was jailed on a charge of possession and circulation of counterfeit money, and later transferred to Chihuahua. He was confined in a cell and was very despondent, as he was sure that he would be killed. I tried to convince him that there was no such danger, that all they wanted was his money. He was liberated not long after I was, but they kept his money.

One day, just as my wife brought my midday lunch, Sam Dreben, a Russian Jew soldier of fortune who had been fighting in the successive revolutions and was acting as an agent for Villa in El Paso, brought in a party of ten newspaper folks to see me, including Bud Fisher and his wife. Dreben was taking them down to Zacatecas to see Villa, who was making his headquarters there, fighting Carranza.[9] One day Mrs. Luz Villa, Villa's first and legitimate wife, gave a banquet for the prisoners in the patio, and a lot of the ladies of the town came and served it, and a military band played. I have

[MISSING PAGE]

to be issued. This warrant had never been served, but was still in effect. He went at once to Mr. Lansing, and suggested that this man be notified that, if I was not at liberty within twenty-four hours, he would be arrested on that old warrant. Mr. Lansing demurred, saying that it was beneath the dignity of the State

Department to resort to such tactics, but my friend insisted, and finally Mr. Lansing reluctantly consented. It worked like a charm. The agent was notified and immediately wired Villa, who wired Chihuahua to have me released at once.

After a few days my Mexican engineer friend who had urged me to pay the money came to see me for the government, and asked me to try to get the money for the ore from the zinc smelting company, which had up to that time ignored me entirely. I wrote, urging them to pay the amount I estimated to be the value of the ore under their contract, with an added amount to cover what I thought to be the expense of the delay and of my arrest. They answered and refused to pay anything. I wired them a threatening message, and they agreed to pay as I suggested, but only through the U.S. State Department, to which I agreed. After about a month the consul received the money, and paid it to the mine manager, who dismissed a suit for damages he had brought against me in the civil court for $100,000, and secured a statement from the judge of the penal court certifying that I was an innocent man [and] should never have been arrested.

After I was released, the consul told me that the military governor, a few days before, had told him that he had received orders from Villa to have me shot. But he did not want to shoot any Americans, just when Villa was especially anxious to secure Wilson's good will and recognition as de-facto ruler of Mexico, so he was going to ignore the order. It took a lot of nerve or assurance to ignore an order of Villa, as he had a way of shooting people who displeased him, without compunction or warning.

About this time President Wilson notified the warring factions in Mexico that he would recognize as the de-facto ruler of Mexico whichever faction would subscribe to certain things which he stated. Villa and all his generals hastened to write letters agreeing to comply with the terms of recognition as stated, while Carranza virtually defied Wilson, and refused to agree to his stipulations. Villa confidently expected to be recognized.

But Americans in Villa territory received a very urgent confidential warning from the State Department, telling them that conditions were such that they [were] likely soon to be in great danger, and virtually ordered them to quietly and quickly get out of the country. So we almost all got out in a hurry. All the small mines and all the big mines but one closed down, also the smelter. The one big mine still running moved its office to El Paso, and left only Mexicans at the mine. I left my house with a Chinaman to look after it, and left the office open with my assistant, whose father was a Cornish miner and his mother a Mexican, to run it. Soon the word came that Wilson had recognized Carranza as the de-facto ruler of Mexico, in spite of his insulting reply to Wilson's letter.[10] Villa was furious, as might have been expected, and Americans were anathema in Villa territory. After a little while Carranza drove Villa out of Chihuahua and Juárez, but he held all the rest of the State of Chihuahua, and carried on guerrilla warfare: burning bridges, holding up trains, raiding ranches, and, in the meantime, recruiting his forces to recover his lost territory.

About the first of 1916 Carranza persuaded the American mine owners and the smelter people to start up again, guaranteeing them protection. They chartered an old Pullman car in Juárez, which some Villa general had used for his private car and had used pretty badly, to go down to Chihuahua. There were forty-two of us, all destined for Chihuahua or the near vicinity, except eighteen who were going on to Cusihuiriachi, ninety miles west of Chihuahua, to start up Potter Palmer's Mine and mill there.[11] I remember saying how easy it would be for Villa to hold up our train, with its little squad of soldiers, and kill us all.

We were not allowed to carry any arms. We heard a rumor that Villa himself was on the way with a large force to seize the railroad at Moctezuma, where we stopped for lunch. We got to Chihuahua about midnight on a Saturday night. The next morning, when I went down to the Foreign Club, I found an old friend who was in charge of a mine at Cusihuiriachi, and asked him to dinner at my house. He said he thought it was foolish to start the mines at Cusihuiriachi. He had not been out there for several months, but had some men working under contract who had finished it, so he had to go out and pay them and make a new contract with them. He was taking five thousand pesos in silver to pay them off. He believed that Villa would raid Cusihuiriachi and kill all those Americans, if they went out there and stayed, and he said, "I can finish my business in an hour, and if the train hasn't left on its return trip within that time, I will be on it."

Monday morning a special train left for Cusihuiriachi, preceded by a train of soldiers at some distance, and having in the rear car the eighteen Americans I had come with from El Paso, my old friend, and another American who was working a mine out there. About noon the railroad dispatcher reported that the commander of the military train had stopped at Santa Isabel, about halfway to Cusi, and would not let them go any farther until the next morning; but just before I went home to dinner in the evening I heard a rumor that the train had been held up, and all the Americans killed. It seemed to have no authenticity, so nobody was much disturbed by it. About two o'clock in the morning I was awakened by the telephone, and was told that the rumor was true, and was asked to be at the railroad station early in the morning. They were preparing to send out a train to recover the bodies.

In the morning they had a train of cattle cars made up with a caboose, in which fourteen armed Americans were going, with a big guard of soldiers in the cattle cars. The Americans were short of guns and ammunition, so I went down to the consulate and got my two rifles and a lot of cartridges I had left there at the time of the Orozco scare. When I got back, I found that the sole survivor of the massacre had come in on horseback, confirmed the story, and gone down town. Later I met him down town, and he told me how he escaped.[12]

The Villistas, two or three hundred of them, under command of Colonel Pablo López, had derailed a locomotive, so the train had to stop, with a bank about as high as the car windows along the left side, and the ground sloping gently on the right side down to the Santa Isabel River nearby. Four of the

Americans went out of the back door of the car and along the left side of the train toward the engine, and, when they were along side their car, about a dozen men rose from concealment at the top of the bank and commenced shooting at them. They turned and fled. This man, being the last, rounded the end of the train first, stumbled, and fell across the track, and the others passed him, running toward the stream. He lay still while the Mexicans went past him, shooting at the other three, all of whom they killed as they ran, and paying no attention to him. After they passed, he crawled behind some bushes and down to the stream, following it until he found a hole, into which he crawled and stayed until the Villistas left. He was near enough to hear the commotion and shouting as they took the others off the train, and shot and bayoneted and clubbed them to death alongside of it. When they were gone he went down the stream until he came to a road leading to Chihuahua, and followed until about midnight, when he struck a ranch, but the people were very unfriendly, and he was afraid they would kill him, so he went on to the next ranch, where they were sympathetic, fed him, lent him a horse to ride and a *sombrero* and *zarape*, and two of them went with him to show him the way.[13]

That day a lot of volunteers made the coffins for the victims, in the shop of a lumber company near the Northwestern station, and an American doctor prepared to embalm the bodies. About three o'clock the next morning one of the relief squads, which had gone after the bodies, telephoned me from down town that they had come in with the bodies, and asked me to go to the station to help my grocer friend guard them, which I did.

About daylight the car was switched into the yard of the lumber company. The doctor came to embalm the bodies but found that it was too late, so four of us, who knew them all but one and could identify them, put them into the coffins and marked them. It was a gruesome task. They were lying in several inches of manure in a cattle car, most of the clothes and all the shoes stripped off them. The man who had had dinner with me Sunday had been shot through the right eye, and had evidently died instantly. Most of the others were not so fortunate, having been shot two or three times, and some of them bayoneted. One had been shot through the hips as he sat in the car, and he was carried out and set on the end of a tie and his brains dashed out with a rifle butt.

When the bodies were in the coffins, the car was switched over to the National Railway, where the coffins were transferred to a waiting train, which left at once for El Paso. I have never seen hostility to Americans so plainly displayed as by the crowd that gathered to see that transfer. Chihuahua was held by Carranza, but there were thousands of Villa secret partisans there. There was no shouting nor rock throwing, but plenty of hostile looks and gestures, and low-voiced unfriendly talk. The next day I was notified that at a meeting of the managers of the principal mines and the smelter it had been decided that conditions were unfavorable for trying to re-open, and they were going to charter a special train to leave from the smelter early the next morning. So I packed my four trunks that I had brought down, and sent them out to the smelter.

I was a partner in a lease on the "Americana" mine at Terrazas, about thirty miles north of Chihuahua, and I thought I ought to warn my partner who was working the mine, and give him a chance to get out with the rest of us. So I found an American who kept a hotel, and was not going to leave, who would take me in his auto early next morning to warn my partner and the master mechanic of the Rio Tinto Copper Mine at Terrazas, who was getting their smelter ready to start up. We got off before daylight, but had hardly passed the picket lines when the motor began to miss, and so we were [delayed] until after seven o'clock reaching Terrazas, where the master mechanic said he was not afraid, and would not go. My partner was down in the mine, and there was no one to let me down with the hoist, so I had to go down the ladderway, and when I found my partner, he said, "I'm not afraid. We've got some good ore, and I'm going to stay and get it out. If Villa comes, I can hide in the mine, and he can never find me."

When I came out, I heard the locomotive whistle blowing at the station, about two miles away, and they waited and tooted until I got there. In El Paso, my other partner, who was the mine superintendent of the Rio Tinto Mine, and who held the lease on the Americana in his name alone, said, "That fellow's crazy. Villa will catch him and kill him sure. We must get him out of there." So he wired him that his presence was needed at once in El Paso, on some pretext, and when he came he told him that he would not consent to his working the lease until he himself felt it safe to go back, and would not furnish any money for expenses until then. The other man was very indignant. He had no money, and saw a chance to make some, so he appealed to me and said, "We've got good ore there, and I'm going to get it out, if I have to walk back, and to borrow the money. When you were at the mine you promised me that you would help me, and you have got to keep your promise." This was true, so I got a sack-full of Mexican pesos at the bank, and he went back. He shipped out two carloads of good ore to me at El Paso, and had nearly finished loading three more, when he got caught in a cave-in and was killed.

After a while a Mexican proposed that we start up again with him in charge, giving him a share in the profits in place of salary. My partner said, "I won't have anything to do with anything I can't look after myself. Besides, this fellow is a thief; he would rob us blind." He offered to turn the lease over to me, if I wanted to work it, so I took it over, and sent the Mexican down to work it. I sent him a check once a week to Chihuahua, where he paid bills and got supplies for another week, and paid the men as soon as he got back to the mine, and hid the supplies down in the mine. So when the Villistas came on a raid, which they did now and then, the most they got was about fifty pesos. We worked this way for three years or more, during which time I was at the mine only once.

Three of us refugees from Chihuahua, who had been associated in some business dealings, seeing that the prospects of returning to Chihuahua to live were somewhat remote, rented an office together, to have a place to do business. Then Villa himself with a large force in the night attacked Columbus, New Mexico, on the line between Mexico and the United States, and eighteen or twenty people were killed in the raid, mostly civilians.[14] Villa was driven off and pursued a long distance into Mexico by the troops at Columbus, and an expedition to capture him was organized, with General Pershing, Commandant at Fort Bliss, in command.[15] I used to see him often, as his offices were in the same building where we had our office, and I often rode in the elevator with him. I thought him an ideal figure of a soldier, not given to much talk, but with plenty of action.[16]

Then there came a pouring into El Paso of seventy thousand National Guardsmen, to be encamped on the desert sands adjacent to Fort Bliss in the blistering heat of June. Most of them had very little experience with outdoor life and were not used to this arid country. They were mostly clerks, bookkeepers, salesmen, mechanics, and the like, and it was a hard experience for them. There was a strong prejudice here against enlisted men in the army, as the regular army is largely recruited from a pretty hard lot of young fellows, and with saloons wide open in town, they did not always behave very well. Many old timers would have no acquaintance nor social contact with the rank and file of the army.

But my wife was sorry for these boys, and often invited some of them to the house and got girls to come and make it pleasant for them. The culmination of these gatherings was a party on Christmas day, with twenty-five boys there and as many girls, which crowded our little house almost to bursting. It was the worst day I have ever seen in El Paso: a heavy snowstorm with a roaring gale, which blew away many tents and demolished some of the galvanized-iron buildings at the camps. Some of the boys could hardly get to my house, but they had a good time. We formed friendships among them which have lasted until now, and we get letters every Christmas yet from some of them.[17]

The Pershing Expedition was doomed to failure, but it proved the ability of the commander. He could have gone to Mexico

City and taken possession of it with that little force, if he had been ordered to do so.

About this time a Mexican who had a little trunk factory in Chihuahua heard that manganese was very valuable in the U.S. He leased a manganese mine near Chihuahua, which had operated a little while some years before, shipping to a steel works at Monterrey, but could not make it pay. He shipped a carload to El Paso, but could find no buyer for it, so he appealed to me, and I bought it. I think that this was the first manganese ore ever shipped out of Mexico. From this I developed quite a business in manganese ore, buying it from producers in Mexico and the Southwest, and mining from properties I acquired in that region by lease or ownership. This did not last very long. The bottom dropped out of manganese prices toward the end of 1918, just before the armistice. If I had not secured a contract for a year about that time, at the prevailing high price, I should have had to quit the manganese business suddenly, as did most of those who rushed into the business. But the government reimbursed them very generously for any losses they claimed. One of them, whose ore I bought, advancing him money to get his ore out, as he never had any money, who got a nice check from the government, failed to get out the last carload for which I advanced the money, or to return the money when he got his check.

After the Santa Isabel massacre I went to Chihuahua only when business urgently required it. Trains were very irregular and uncertain, and might be held up any time by Villistas, and some of the passengers killed. If Villa happened to be there himself, he might spy someone for whom he had a dislike, or who had offended him, and he would take pleasure in shooting him himself. My agent in Chihuahua wrote me that a Mexican tailor had told him of some good manganese that was open to location, and I went down to take a look at it. I found that it was about forty-five miles west of town, in Villa territory, within sight of the big cave in the Sierra de la Silla (Saddle Mountain) where Villa had made his headquarters when he was a bandit. My man said everything was quiet out there, and we would have no trouble; so I hired an Italian with a Model T touring car, and went out with the Mexican, my French agent, and the Italian driver.[18]

The manganese was good, so I took samples, we ate our lunch, and, just as we started to get into the car, there came from every direction a yelling crowd of Villistas on horseback. One especially black and dirty one, whose hair stuck up through a hole in his hat, rushed up at me and stuck a .45 gun under my nose, and yelled, "You !@#$ gringo, I'm going to blow your brains out." He was evidently pretty drunk, and I thought he would do it. It is an uncomfortable feeling when you think your last second has come. That gun looked as big as a cannon. But he didn't shoot. They searched us, and found a pistol in the car, which the driver acknowledged belonged to him, but he produced a permit from the Carranza authorities to carry it. The Captain said that was to no avail there, and he would be shot for having that pistol. They put the Frenchman and the Mexican on two of their horses, and two of them got in the back seat with me and one in front with the chauffeur, and had him drive across country to the base of the Sierra de la Silla, about five miles away.

On the way one of my guards told me cheerfully that they would shoot us all after we got over to headquarters. We got stuck in the sand, crossing an arroyo, and I had a chance to hide my checkbook and fountain pen and notebook under a rock. I was afraid that the checkbook and pen might suggest a check for ransom. The fellow that had searched me had kept my watch and a plain gold ring I wore, but the watch was a dollar one, as I had left my good watch in town. These men were under the command of Martín López, brother of Pablo López, who was in command at the Santa Isabel massacre, and he was said to be a worse gringo-hater than Pablo; but Martín had gone to Durango to see Villa, and left a colonel in command.

When we got to the foot of the mountain we had to stop, and a man went up to the cave to bring the colonel down.

While we waited our captors told us their troubles. They said they were not fighters by choice, but peaceable ranchers who lived in the vicinity, whose ranches the Carranza soldiers periodically raided, carrying off their livestock and farm products and ravishing their women. So they joined the Villa army, and made their headquarters at the cave through the day, and went home to sleep at night.

When the colonel came, he was very reasonable. He said they were not bandits, and would not rob us, and when I told him what I was there for and explained that the manganese ore would be of no value to them, under conditions then prevailing, he said, "Go ahead and work. We have plenty of horses and wagons, and will haul the ore to the railroad as cheaply as anyone, and we need the money." So they let us go, and showed us the way to the road, and we got back to town about nine o'clock that night. My agent located the ground, and sent the tailer to work it, and he hired those Villistas to do the work and haul the ore. The only trouble I had was with Carranzista soldiers, who would commandeer the cars, which I had, with much difficulty, gotten at Palomas to load ore into, and to use them to haul hay for the army. I sent the Colonel a three-dollar watch, and he was very friendly and helpful. The next day I went with my agent to look at a manganese prospect he had leased for me and was working, about fifteen miles north of town. My man said, "It's all quiet out there where we are going, so surely we won't have any trouble to-day."

The road was very rocky. Instead of an auto we got a man with a shiny new spring wagon with a canvas cover, and the finest pair of sleek black Spanish mules I ever saw, with new harnesses decorated with silver. I found that the prospect was no good, so we did not stay long, and were well on our way back, almost within sight of the city, when two men on horseback with rifles held us up. They took the mules and harness, my money, new overcoat, coat, and lace boots. When I protested about the boots, the one who took them took off his shoes and gave them to me. But his shoes were about number-thirteen Brogans, and my boots number sevens, to which I called his attention. He said, "Somebody can wear those boots, and they are much better than my shoes." He took my glasses and fountain pen and handkerchief, but returned them when I reminded him that he could not use them, and I could not get along without the glasses.

We set out for town, but it was hard going on that rocky road, my partner being barefoot, and my Brogans hard on the feet. Soon a cart with solid wooden wheels, drawn by three burros, came along, and hitched onto the wagon, which the bandits had not taken, and presently overtook us, and hauled us into town. I went into the first big store I came to, whose proprietors I knew, and got a coat, and thought I might get to my hotel, where I had a pair of shoes, without meeting anyone I knew. But presently I passed my old friend Con O'Callahan, standing in the door of the American barbershop, and he spotted the coat and shoes, and demanded an explanation, and had a good laugh at my expense. I borrowed an overcoat, and took those shoes home with me, to show to my wife.[19]

The next day I went to the Americana Mine. I had to ride in a boxcar to Terrazas, but my man had a wagon at the station there. He said it was about time for another Villista raid, but they did not come while I was there. An American doctor who had been my next-door neighbor, and was still living in Chihuahua, was in touch with Villa's head man in Chihuahua at that time. When I came back from Terrazas I told him I was going home [the] next day, and he said, "Don't go now. Villa is planning a big raid on the railroad in the next few days, and he might get you and shoot you." I said that I had to go, to attend to urgent business. That night at the Club he brought me a little piece of paper with cryptic signs in pencil on it, and told me it was my "safe-conduct" which he had got from Villa's man, and said that if I should get held up, I should present it to the leader of the band, and I should not be molested. The train was not held up, and I have that "salvoconducto" yet.

One of the refugees in the office with me, along with some others, bought a mine about a hundred miles south of El Paso,

Business in the Borderlands

and one day when he and the mine manager were on their way from the mine to the railroad they were held up by a bunch of Villistas, who released the manager to go and get [a] $30,000 ransom for the other man, whom they held. Villa himself came along in a day or two, on a recruiting trip, and traveled around with them, riding horseback all day, never staying two nights in the same place, for a month. Whenever Villa told a man that he was to go with them, he went, or was shot without further ado. The ransom money was arranged for, and Villa and two others brought my friend across the river to El Paso one night and got it. Villa finally recruited his forces up to a reputed thirteen thousand men, and made a surprise attack on Juárez at night. He had possession of most of the town, the Carranza troops having been driven into the citadel at the edge of town, when the commandant at Fort Bliss, on the pretext of stopping firing which was coming across the river into El Paso, sent a detachment of Negro cavalry to drive them out, and some artillery to flank them on the outskirts of Juárez.

They soon drove them off, and the artillery followed them for fifteen or twenty miles, occasionally dropping a shell among them. I watched them from the window of my office, which was in the twelfth story of a building, overlooking the river. That was a hard blow to Villa, and his fortunes waned from that time. He besieged Chihuahua, and made a surprise attack at night, and had possession of almost the whole city, including the public buildings; but the Carranzistas rallied and drove him out and captured about three hundred of his men, all of whom were promptly hanged to a row of big alamo trees along an avenue going down to the river. Ropes seem to have been scarce, as in many cases three were hanged with one rope, and dangled there like a bunch of carrots.

From that time on his forces dwindled, and the Carranzistas chased him around, and finally cornered him and forced him to surrender with about three hundred men. Even then he dictated terms to them, so that they paid him a large sum of money, guaranteed him and his men immunity, let them keep their equipment and horses and arms, and bought a big fine ranch for them all to live on under his supervision, a baronial estate.

It was during that period that the secretary of Hipólito Villa, Pancho Villa's brother, came to see me about disposing of a lot of silver-gold bullion which he was guarding at San Carlos, an isolated village in the northeastern corner of the State of Chihuahua. He said there was about three million ounces of it, pretty rich in gold, and if I could handle it for him, he would give me a fourth of the proceeds. He wanted to bring it across the river at Boquillas, a few miles from San Carlos, where there was a ford, but it was not a port of entry. I was shipping zinc ore from near Boquillas, which had been brought across the river from the Boquillas del Carmen Mine on a tramway, and was paying the salary of a U.S. customs inspector to receive it, and it was loaded on the cars at Marathon, ninety miles from Boquillas.

I consulted with the Customs Collector at El Paso, and wired the Secretary of the Treasury for permission to import the bullion at Boquillas and to use the same inspector that I already had there to receive it, and the Superintendent of the Mint at Denver, to make sure that the bullion would be received there. All seemed to be auspicious. I told Hipólito's man it would be all right and he left, saying that I should hear from him within five days that the bullion was ready to come across. However, the Carranzistas in the meantime descended upon San Carlos with a big force, and Hipólito had to leave in a hurry. So vanished another prospect of making a million or so in a hurry.

For a while after the World War things went well enough with me. The ore in the "Americana" Mine played out, so I had to quit there, but the manganese business lasted a while longer, thanks to the contract I had secured just in the nick of time. Then after the beginning of 1920 nothing seemed to prosper. I kept looking around for a prospect or a mine I might work and make some money out of, but when I found something that looked like it might make a paying proposition and did some work on it, it did not pan out. For three years my resources kept shrinking, until they were almost at the vanishing point, when

I was offered the management of a mine at Cusihuiriachi, at a good salary. This was the same mine that my friend [who] was killed in the Santa Isabel massacre had been managing. I did not want to go to Mexico to live again, but I had to take that job or go broke, so I went.

Cusihuiriachi is a typical Mexican Sierra mining camp. Houses are strung along the banks of a stream at the bottom of a deep gulch for two miles or more, with a crooked, stony, muddy road, where hogs wallowed and cows and burros and goats wandered, following the stream now on one side and now on the other. My stay there was uneventful, the routine of working a mine and shipping ore. There I met again my doctor-assayer friend that I had first met on my second trip into Mexico, he being employed by a mine there in that double capacity.

Another revolution started while I was there, but President Calles, a strong man, soon put it down. About two hundred men volunteered in Cusi for services with the government, but the revolt had been put down before they arrived at the scene of the fighting. After fifteen months I was transferred to Chihuahua City, to look after some mines at Santa Eulalia, fifteen miles southeast of Chihuahua, and at Almoloya, about 150 miles southwest from Chihuahua, which my boss had acquired.[20] Almoloya is the worst place for rattlesnakes I have ever seen. I think I never made a trip to the mine by auto without running over at least one. They even came into the house. After doing about a thousand feet of tunneling and drifting there and failing to find ore in paying quantity, we gave that place up.

In Chihuahua I lived in a two-story brick and adobe house on a corner near the center of town, which had been the rectory of an Episcopal Church adjoining it. It had been a prosperous church, with an American rector, and a good attendance every Sunday until after the revolutions began; then the attendance gradually dwindled until the church died. The same fate overtook the Congregational, Methodist, and Baptist American churches, as their communicants left the country. None of them has resumed services, and it seems unlikely that any of them will ever be revived, as the attitude of all government administrations since the revolutions began has been against religion.[21]

There are also many less Americans and Britishers there than before the revolutions. The Chihuahua Foreign Club, of which I was a charter member, was organized in 1906, and was a prosperous concern until after the revolutions started, but is a mere ghost of its former self, foreign residents being so many less than formerly, and Mexicans having been allowed to become proprietary members.[22] We used the auditorium of the church for a storeroom.

It was about the time I went to Chihuahua from Cusi that Villa was killed.[23] Many a Mexican has said to me during the Villa regime that Villa bore a charmed life, and that no bullet could kill him. He had a house in Parral, a mining town in southern Chihuahua not far from his ranch, where he lived a good deal of the time. The assassins, about ten of them, rented a house on a corner, where he turned toward the center of town, which gave them a clear view of [the] house, so they could see him whenever he started to town. As he turned the corner in his auto, they all started firing from the doorway and windows and roof, and riddled Villa and his three companions before they could fire a shot. Then the killers mounted their horses and rode away unmolested. It was freely intimated that President Calles was the instigator of this deed, as Villa, with his band of veteran revolutionists, all equipped, was a constant menace to any government. Anyhow, I think the killers were never punished, although later, the leader, who was a deputy in the national Congress, openly boasted of it.[24]

In 1927 I took a vacation, and my wife and I took a leisurely trip to New York, visiting along the way, and got there just the day before Lindbergh set forth for Paris.[25] We went to the Roxy Theatre that evening, and his flight was announced from the stage, but there seemed little excitement; that did not appear until news of his successful arrival came. Next year my wife went to Ruidoso, New Mexico, where my son-in-law has a summer cabin, to spend the summer.

Business in the Borderlands

One day when I was eating my lunch at the Hotel Palacio, the sister-in-law of the man who got me out of the penitentiary, who was there settling up his estate, came in and sat down with me. She said, "You need a vacation. I have made some money in the stock market, and I want to do some good with it. If you will go on a vacation with it, I will give you $150 of it." I took the money and went off to Catalina Island and had a good time for three weeks.

I had my first airplane ride there. It was a little one-seater seaplane, the pilot taking two passengers on the seat with him. The other passenger was a young fellow, who said to the pilot, "I want to get a kick out of this. I have been up a lot of times, so it's nothing new to me." So the pilot did a lot of stunts that kept my heart in my mouth, the worst of which was diving from two thousand feet or so until it seemed that we were certain to go straight down into the water; but he flattened out just in time, so near the water that I could see the fish swimming around.

Life moved along tranquilly at the leisurely Mexican pace for five years or so. Then, my boss took over an old silver mine about 125 miles northwest of El Paso, in New Mexico. I had to divide my time between Chihuahua and El Paso, and my wife went back to El Paso, so that she could be with my daughter while I was away.

Pretty soon, while I was on one of my sojournings in Chihuahua, another revolution started there. One of the leaders was General Caraveo, Governor of the State of Chihuahua, and a veteran of all the revolutions, having been a general in the Madero revolution and in every one afterward, except the abortive one while I was at Cusi.[26] This one did not last long. There was only one important battle, at Jiménez in southern Chihuahua. The federal airmen blew up a carload of dynamite, which spelled havoc for the rebels. General Escobar, who headed the revolution, decamped soon after that, and made his getaway with plenty of funds to Montreal, where I think he is still, and left General Caraveo to conduct the evacuation of Chihuahua City.

I got caught in Chihuahua, with no way to get to El Paso, where I was due, trains having been discontinued. Then I heard that Caraveo had a train standing ready at the railroad shops across the river, to take him and his rear guard to Juárez. So I hurried over there and found the train and boarded it, and pretty soon another American came and got on. Caraveo and his staff came in an hour or so, but waited another hour or more, until a messenger came on horseback. Then he gave the order to go. At Agua Nueva, seventy-five miles to the north, the rear guard of four hundred men, with their horses and equipment, were loaded onto the empty cars. At Laguna there was a long wooden bridge, and the train waited while they poured kerosene on it and set it afire. After that all long wooden bridges or trestles were fired, and more and more of Caraveo's men got on board along the way, so we were from about noon until daylight the next morning getting to Juárez. But it was a club car on which we were travelling, so they fed us. Caraveo came over to El Paso, where he lived for several years, when he received amnesty, and went back to Chihuahua.

These frequently recurring revolutions since 1910 have done Mexico incalculable harm, and reduced it from a rich and prosperous and progressive country, with a stable and liberal government, to a poverty-stricken country, with a radical and bankrupt government.[27] The workers, for whose benefit these revolutions are supposed to have been fought, are no better off today than they were before, in spite of all the laws and edicts in their favor, and especially designed to discriminate against foreigners. "Mexico for Mexicans" has been their principal slogan, and they are not far from achieving that end.

When the Madero revolution began, Mexico was overrun with foreigners looking for investments in land, mining, industry, and merchandizing. Foreign money was pouring into the country, and the foreign population was much greater than it is now, and rapidly increasing in numbers and quality. There was a scarcity of labor, especially in the mining business, and wages were steadily rising. Americans usually treated their employees better than others, and paid better wages and salaries. With the fairest and most liberal mining law in the world, the mining business was booming, wages were rising, and the federal treasury was receiving a big revenue from the production of the mines.

Now prospective investors are few in any line. With a restrictive mining law, high taxes and laws favoring labor, most small mines have had to close, and many of the large ones have shut down or turned over to the workmen to operate, with the backing of the government or its encouragement. Soon after the collapse of the Escobar revolution we relinquished the mines we had been working in Santa Eulalia, and I came back to El Paso to live.[28]

We were doing some exploration work on a famous old silver mine in New Mexico, from which several million dollars' worth of ore had been produced in a short time, from a depth of less than a hundred feet below the surface. The ore had been cut off by a fault, and a geologist who had a very high reputation, especially regarding this particular type of ore occurrence, persuaded my boss that chances were good that with a little work we might pick up the rich ore again where it had been cut off. We soon found the ore in all four places where it had been lost, but it was too low in value to ship. As we worked in on it, it grew steadily poorer instead of better. After giving it a thorough tryout, we had to give it up.

I went scouting around for something that looked like it might pay to work and after a time we decided to try a copper mine in the Burro Mountains near Tyrone, New Mexico. Tyrone is a model mining town, built by a great copper-mining company at a cost of several million dollars, with its own standard gauge railroad and fine terminal station, big department store, schools, hotel, water works, light plant, and houses for all the employees—from manager to mine mucker—handsome, substantial, comfortable, convenient, and artistic. It is in a national forest, which is also a federal game preserve, where deer and turkeys and quail wander in security through the woods, and even live in town.

Many years ago the mining company stopped operations, but it maintains the town, renting the houses with water and light. It is an ideal summer resort, never hot, although the altitude is not very great. I had a nice house there, with practically all city conveniences. A telephone connected with the Bell system at Silver City thirteen miles away, at a lower cost than my telephone here. The ice man and the milk man [came] every morning, also the baker. It had electric light with lots of sockets to plug into all over the house, and a big fireplace in the living room, with plenty of nice smelly cedar wood for chilly evenings in rainy weather. Unfortunately the mine did not turn out very well, so we gave it up and did some work on a gold-silver-copper-lead mine thirteen miles from Tyrone at White Signal.

This mine had a big vein of the hardest white quartz I have ever seen, with no deep workings, which, at less than ten feet from the surface, showed combined values of the four metals almost enough to give a profit. The shaft continued down alongside the vein to a depth of forty feet, and I thought maybe it would be worthwhile to run a crosscut from the bottom of the shaft across the vein, to see if the values at that depth increased enough to be profitable. They remained the same, however, so I gave that place up, and left Tyrone with regret.

The next spring, out on the desert in Arizona, I found two old mines adjoining each other, each of which had a pile of ore on the dump, which my samples indicated was good milling ore. I took them over on a contract of lease and option to buy, had the ore on the dumps shipped to the smelter to see how it would turn out, and had the old workings thoroughly sampled, to see if that ore could be found underground. The 133 tons of ore shipped to the smelter showed an average value of $9.50 a ton in gold, and the sampling underground indicated that there was enough of it showing in the workings to warrant the expense of building a mill to treat it.

It takes a good deal of water to treat ore in a mill. One of the mines had a lot of water standing in the old workings, but I could not find out if the watercourse which supplied it fur-

Business in the Borderlands

nished enough to keep a mill running without pumping out the mine and measuring it, which would cost quite a lot of money. Knowing that I could get enough water from a well four miles away, if the water in the mine was not sufficient, I took a chance and built the mill. When I started the mill, I soon found that the water was not enough to supply it, and I had run out of money. I could not equip the well with pump and pipeline, and on account of the Depression it seemed impossible for me to get the money. I gave it up and sold the equipment. I suppose that some day those mines will be worked and yield a profit.

Notes

1. The United States Navy, under orders from President Woodrow Wilson, occupied the port of Veracruz from April through November 1914, in part responding to the Tampico Affair, and also prompted by a shipment of German arms to Huerta. Knight writes that the "landing was expected to be rapid, limited and virtually bloodless. It was in no sense a preamble to a full-scale intervention, which Wilson unequivocally opposed." Nevertheless, tensions between the United States and Mexico escalated. Knight, *Mexican Revolution*, vol. 2, 152–53.

2. Terrazas Jr filed a statement in 1916 in Los Angeles, quoted in Katz, *Pancho Villa*, 245–46.

3. The house to which Worcester likely refers, where the widow of Pancho Villa continued to live after his death, is "La Quinta Luz" and is today El Museo Histórico de la Revolución. The original site and building was purchased by Villa previously, though he expanded and remodeled it after 1914. "Museo Histórico de la Revolución," Gobierno de México, http://www.gob.mx/sedena/acciones-y-programas/museo-historico -de-la-revolucion. Last accessed January 30, 2020. My thanks to Noé Casas Rodríguez for guiding me to the museum.

4. El Paso newspapers first reported Worcester's imprisonment on March 3, 1915. The *Herald* claimed he had been held in the Chihuahua penitentiary since February 13. "Villa Officers Hold American," *El Paso Herald*, March 3, 1915, 3; "American Mining Man in Prison at Chihuahua," *El Paso Times*, March 3, 1915, 1. By mid-March, State Department officials were working to identify revolutionary leaders and to appeal for Worcester's release. This would not be completed until later in April. Cobb to Secretary of State, March 18, 1915, RG 59: Records of the Department of State, Central Files, 1910–1929, Mexico, Political Affairs (812.00). Accessed via "Revolution in Mexico, the 1917 Constitution, and Its Aftermath: Records of the U.S. State Department," Archives Unbound (Gale, A Cengage Company). Last accessed February 5, 2019.

5. After the assassination of Madero, Antonio Rábago installed himself as Governor of Chihuahua and deposed his predecessor and associate of Villa's, Abraham González. Following orders from Huerta, Rábago sent González to Mexico City. On the way, González was assassinated. Francisco Naranjo, *Diccionario biográfico revolucionario* (México: Comisión Nacional para las Celebraciones del 125 Aniversario de la Independencia Nacional y 25 Aniversario de la Revolución Mexicana, 1935).

6. The Worcesters, like the U.S. Government, were caught between revolutionary factions. Gertrude reported on this from Chihuahua, writing to her aunt in Leadville, "None of the boys are here, and I don't want them to come. We seem so helpless because of the attitude of our government. They told us we came back at our own risk and Bryan has absolutely no desire to protect or keep Americans or to know the truth. If we know that Uncle Sam ever had done anything or ever would it would not seem so bad. These people here know that he does not want to offend them consequently they will go to any lengths. Now the case has resolved itself into one of extortion nothing else. . . . I can't realize that this thing has happened to us. It seems like a horrible nightmare from which some time I must awaken. A judge in El Paso advised us to stir up as many of the Senators as possible; he thought in that way some action would soon be taken." Gertrude Worcester to Mary Henderson, March 9, 1915, reprinted in "Former Lenox Woman's Husband Held in Mexican Prison for Ransom," *Jefferson Gazette*, March 23, 1915. My thanks to Barbara Hamilton, Dave Martin, and Carrie Wimer for assistance in locating and transcribing this source and others from the same publication.

7. Worcester was close to the Consul, Martin Letcher, but George Carothers reported to the State Department information from Villa's men, effectively delaying Worcester's release on bond or otherwise. This infuriated the mining man's family, which started a press and political campaign by letters and personal contacts to hasten his release. Worcester's son, Herbert, issued a statement to the *El Paso Herald*: "I wish to correct a statement made by the state department through special agent George C. Carothers and printed in your paper, to the effect that my father, Leonard Worcester, jr., has refused bail from the Mexican authorities in Chihuahua, Mexico.

"My father has asked for bail twice and both times has been refused. The last time was on the 12th instant, to Diaz Lombardo, minister of justice (?) who absolutly [sic] refused to let him give bond under any conditions.

"G.C. Carothers absolutely ignored the statement of the case made to him by Mr. Letcher, American consul at Chihuahua, and, instead, sent the statement of the case as represented by the Hon. Diaz Lombardo to the department at Washington. Of course as Mr. Carothers has evidently a great respect for Villa and his band, he does not dare incur their enmity by trying to obtain, for a fellow countryman, justice which is due.

"I also wish to state that it is through no fault of his that my father is held a prisoner, but through the fault of the Granby Smelting and Refining company in not fulfilling its contract." "Statement from Worcester," *El Paso Herald*, March 25, 1915, 16; see also "Angeles Slated to Be President," *Marion Daily Star*, March 24, 1915, 2.

8. William Jennings Bryan.

9. Journalist and editor John Wheeler traveled on this trip with Fisher, Dreben, Gunther Lessing, and Floyd Gibbons, among others, narrated with slightly different details, in his "They Never Tell—ALL," *The American Magazine* 112, no. 6 (December 1931), 36–38, 80.

10. The United States officially recognized the Carranza-led government on October 19, 1915. See esp. Peter V. N. Henderson, "Woodrow Wilson, Victoriano Huerta, and the Recognition Issue in Mexico," *The Americas* 41, no. 2 (October 1984).

11. Potter Palmer Jr. owned the "Promontorio mine and other claims" at Cusihuiriachi in 1920. Walter Harvey Weed, *The Mines Handbook: An Enlargement of the Copper Handbook* 14 (New York: Weed, 1920), 1674.

12. The Santa Isabel massacre, perpetrated by General Pablo López (and likely ordered by Villa), killed seventeen American mining engineers, one of the most flagrant outbursts of targeting Americans in the revolutionary era. Two months later Villa would attack Columbus, New Mexico. Relatively little has focused exclusively on the Santa Isabel, or Santa Ysabel, massacre. See Miguel Antonio Levario, *Militarizing the Border: When Mexicans Became the Enemy* (College Station: Texas A&M University Press, 2012), 38–52; Jason T. Darrah, "Anglos, Mexicans, and the San Ysabel Massacre: A Study of Changing Ethnic Relations in El Paso, Texas, 1910–1916" (MA thesis, Texas Tech University, 2003); and John S. D. Eisenhower, *Intervention! The United States and the Mexican Revolution, 1913–1917* (New York: Norton, 1995).

13. This was Thomas B. Holmes, whose affidavit is quoted in Katz, *Pancho Villa*, 558.

14. March 8–9, 1916.

15. John J. Pershing.

16. Knight describes the Pershing expedition as a "hasty, ill-prepared, muddled and—from the perspective of American domestic politics—unavoidable response to Villa's aggression." Knight, *Mexican Revolution*, vol. 2, 347; see also Katz, *Pancho Villa*, 567–70.

17. The *El Paso Herald* confirms Worcester's memory of this snowstorm and its effects on the military encampment: "A great Christmas celebration, prepared for the field headquarters camp here, was spoiled late Monday when the worst storm yet experienced in this region descended and swept the military encampment from end to end. Swirling down the chimneys of the adobe shacks, the wind filled the dwellings with smoke which drove officers and men into the open until the hearth and stove fires could be extinguished. Tents were flattened, adobe houses unroofed and kitchen fires blown away." "Storm Damages Pershing's Camp," *El Paso Herald*, December 26, 1916, 1.

18. March 1918.

19. This anecdote squares with a report from the American Consul, J. B. Stewart, from March 24, 1918: "In company with a Frenchman, a Mexican and a chauffeur [Worcester] drove to a point about 45 miles South-West of Chihuahua and 15 miles South of Palomas, a station on the Mexican Northwestern Railway. Here they were held up by a group of bandits who claimed they were Martin Lopez men, followers of Villa. They were carefully questioned by the officer in charge and Mr. Worcester frankly told him that he was a mining man with undeveloped mines nearby and that he had come out to look over his property which he wanted to develop. Taken to the mine the men became convinced of their good intentions and became very cordial. Not only did they not rob Mr. Worcester and his companions but they took pains to assure them that they were not bandits and were interested only in the protection of their property and in the development of the country. They insisted that the real bandits were the federal troops who, they said, were in the habit of looting their ranches whenever they came to the neighborhood.

"Mr. Worcester was impressed with the sincerity of the men and believed that, while they claimed to be followers of Villa, they were inspired by motives the same as those of the men organized under the name of 'Defensa Social'—ranchers associated in various parts to protect their property against federal as well as Villa troops.

"The next day Mr. Worcester had another experience but this time with common bandits and only about 3 miles from the center of the city. With the same companions, except the chauffeur, he was returning, about four in the afternoon, from a visit to a prospect located about 15 miles Northeast of town, when the party was suddenly covered by bandits. They were quickly robbed and relieved of most of their clothing. The Mexican driver lost a good team of mules and all had to return to the city on foot.

"What impressed Mr. Worcester to-day was the contrast between the two groups—the latter common, roving bandits, the former ranchers opposed to the present Government and followers of Villa. These ranchers, I neglected to state above, also assured Mr. Worcester that they would assist him in every way in the development of his property, urged him to start work and guaranteed protection to him and his workmen." Stewart to Secretary of State, March 24, 1918, RG 59.

20. *The Lead and Zinc News* locates the Almoloya district near Parral, or 150 miles southeast, rather than southwest, of Chihuahua. *The Lead and Zinc News* 12, no. 10 (January 14, 1907), 11.

21. Worcester describes a dwindling of "American churches" in Chihuahua with the return of U.S. citizens north of the border, but this does not correspond with a larger history of American missionaries there. Protestant missionaries had success in the region; for example, a Methodist church that continues in Chihuahua City today—*La Santísima Trinidad*, from which Worcester himself witnessed early revolutionary skirmishes—was started by American Congregational missionaries.

22. Claude Rice noted in 1908 that the Chihuahua Foreign Club had "200 members (full quota) and a large number on the waiting list" and was "composed mostly of mining men." "The Ore Deposits of Santa Eulalia, Mexico," *The Engineering and Mining Journal* 85, no. 25 (June 20, 1908), 1.

23. July 20, 1923.

24. A deputy to the state legislature of Durango, Jesús Salas Barraza, confessed to the killing of Villa. The assassin "described himself as the avenger of thousands of Villa's victims, as a man driven solely by his conscience to the point of disregarding 'the consequences that this act could have for his poor children.'" Katz, *Pancho Villa*, 772–73.

25. The famous aviator Charles Lindbergh first soared to fame in 1927 when he completed a solo flight nonstop from New York City to Paris.

26. Marcelo Caraveo was a military zone commander who rose as Governor of Chihuahua in 1928 and joined Escobar's revolution the following year. When it failed, he sought exile in El Paso. Mark Wasserman, *Persistent Oligarchs: Elites and Politics in Chihuahua, Mexico, 1910–1940* (Durham: Duke University Press, 1993), 41.

27. Worcester again has a very pessimistic view of the value of the Mexican Revolution. His views certainly differ from Mexican workers and laboring classes who benefited from land redistribution and *ejidos* with the administration of Lázaro Cárdenas in 1934. Worcester's opinion is representative of an entire generation (and class) of American businessmen who had bet their futures on an underregulated Mexican mining industry.

28. Escobar's short-lived rebellion ended in May 1929.

6

Coda

THE FIRST SUMMER THAT I HAD THAT MINE MY WIFE AND I took a vacation trip in the car to Colorado, to visit old haunts and see old friends. We ambled along up the Rio Grande, stopping at Socorro, Santa Fe, and Taos in New Mexico, and at Creede in Colorado, following the river to its very source at Wolf Creek Pass; then on to Durango, from there over the "Million Dollar Highway" through the San Juan mining district to Grand Junction; then to Steamboat Springs, Leadville, Cripple Creek, and Colorado Springs. We came through Kokomo, where I worked so many years before, and there were several houses in seemingly good condition, but I did not see any sign of habitation. All seemed deserted. But at Climax, a few miles from there, we passed the great Climax Molybdenum Company's mine, which is literally a mountain of ore, and produces most of the molybdenum used in the world at present. This mine was originally owned by two brothers who belonged to my Drum Corps in Leadville.

I was much surprised at the prosperous appearance of Leadville. I had expected to find a "ghost" town, but there were still more than 3,500 people living there. The town seemed lively and the houses well kept, and the people cheerful and contented. This was a contrast to the apparent general attitude of the people of Cripple Creek, where they most all seemed depressed, and croaked about the hard times, although the camp was producing three or four million dollars in gold that year. I could think of only two people whom I knew that still lived in Leadville, but the next day, after we arrived, there were twenty-five or thirty old friends who came to see us after an absence of thirty-eight years.

A strange thing happened there. When the Drum Corps was in Boston in 1891, I had a photograph taken by Elmer Chickering, with me seated in the center, a big picture eighteen by twenty-four inches in size, which was framed and kept with the belongings of the Drum Corps.[1] The first evening we were in Leadville we took a walk down the main street, and when we passed the Tabor Opera House, there in the middle of the window of one of the store rooms on the ground floor, all alone, was that picture. I wondered how it happened to be there, as no one knew that we were coming. The explanation was simple: the custodian of the Opera House was an old Drum Corps boy who was also custodian of the effects of the defunct Drum Corps, which he had stored in a vacant storeroom. When he cleared out the storeroom for a new tenant, he picked up the picture off the floor and put it in the window, to get it out of the way.

I suppose Cripple Creek seemed so much more quiet because it had still been lively when I left there. Now, they are going to drive a new drainage tunnel, thirty-two thousand feet long and one thousand feet deeper than the old Roosevelt tunnel, borrowing $1 million or more from the RFC.[2] This will probably give the old camp a long lease of life. The old town looks like a ghost, but it is a pretty lively spook. I think the mines produced $4 million or more last year. A man who had been my assistant at the Moose Mine came to see me there. After I left there, he made some money on a lease on one of the mines and went to Tucson, Arizona, where he bought an irrigated farm, where he did well until the Depression came, and then it looked like he might lose it. He went back to Cripple Creek, got a lease on the same old mine, and was doing well, so he seemed likely to save his farm.

I did not know nearly so many people in Cripple Creek as in Leadville, although I had been gone eleven years longer from

Leadville, and I had been very well acquainted in Cripple Creek. When things began to go bad with the three railroads that terminated at Cripple Creek, a banker there bought up one of them, the Cripple Creek Short Line, to Colorado Springs, and sold the right-of-way to a man who made it into a toll-road. It is a very good road, with no grades that are steep for an auto, and one can coast almost every foot of the way to Colorado Springs.

At Colorado Springs, of course, we had to drive up to the top of Pike's Peak and look down on old Cripple Creek from there. When I lived in Cripple Creek, I had gone up to the top of the peak horseback with my father-in-law, when he was visiting me, and from my office window at the Moose I could see the cog train climb the peak.[3]

From Colorado Springs we went to Denver for only a few hours, and then had a leisurely drive home, stopping at Pueblo, Las Vegas, Santa Rosa, Roswell, the Carlsbad Caverns, and finally at Pine Springs in the Guadalupe Mountains. I think that was the most enjoyable trip I ever took: perfect weather all the way, no mishaps but a flat tire or two, and I always had a spare ready. The Carlsbad Caverns are a stupendous and beautiful wonder.

The next year we drove to the Grand Canyon of Arizona, stopping on the way to see the Petrified Forest, the Painted Desert, and Meteor Crater. A log turned to stone is no great wonder, but a whole forest of giant trees turned to onyx of almost gem-like beauty, with all the colors of the rainbow, is something I could hardly even imagine. The huge bowl of the Painted Desert has been liberally splashed with the bright colors of the Grand Canyon.

When I saw the great pit, five hundred feet deep and a mile in diameter, made by the impact of that meteor in the fraction of a second in solid rock, and compared it with the great open pit copper mine at Santa Rita, New Mexico, somewhere about the same size, the product of the efforts of an army of men with mechanical drills, dynamite, and steam shovels for more than twenty-five years, I was glad I was not in that vicinity when the meteor landed.

I suppose the Grand Canyon is the most stupendous and colorful and awe-inspiring spectacle in the world. At least it gives me the impression of being unapproachable by anything I could possibly imagine. It seems to me that it must be the same of the World's natural spectacles.

From Grand Canyon we went down by Prescott to the mine, in western Arizona in the mountainous desert, where [the] summer temperature is often 115 and sometimes 120, and where once there was no rain at the mine for eighteen months. It is called a desert, but it is far from it. Vegetation grows thick over most of it, and when it rains the valleys are green. There are even a good many trees, the ironwoods and Palo Verdes covered with a mass of flowers in the springtime. There is much animal life, from insects to deer, and many cattle roam the valleys and hillsides, this being the principal business of the region. Flowers are abundant, every cactus bearing blossoms, even the giant saguaro cactus, which grows here to a height of more than twenty-five feet. There are many birds. Four funny little owls used to come and perch together in the ironwood trees by the house in the evening, many white-winged doves lived around there, a big covey of quail lived near the house, and went close by every day as they went foraging down toward the valley. When there is water enough to water it, farm produce thrives.

I had very good cantaloupes at Christmas time, from a garden not far from the mine. Living was not hard there, except for the heat. It was only eight minutes by auto down to the village, where the international paved highway passed through, so every morning the milk-ice truck came through from Wickenburg, fifty miles away. The hucksters and traveling groceries came from as far away as Los Angeles. The nearby garden supplied fresh vegetables. What with gas refrigerator and air conditioning, the heat even could be much alleviated. I was sorry to have to give that mine up.

My second son, who is a mining engineer, was superintendent of a mine in the Bradshaw Mountains, and he and an old-time Cripple Creeker that I knew took a lease on a little old mine about five miles away called the "Little Joe." They offered to let me in on it, if I wanted to come in, which I did. The other man looked after the place, and we worked along in a small way for a year or so, but could not make it pay, so we quit it. In the meantime, as usual, I kept looking round trying to find something to work on and have kept on doing so ever since, but without success.

Every now and then somebody offers me something, and if it sounds like it might be good, I go and look at it. I have looked at a lot of prospects and old workings, but haven't found one I want to work. Yesterday a woman called me up and told me she had some claims in eastern Arizona, on which her deceased husband had driven two tunnels, one seven hundred feet long and the other four hundred feet, looking for the vein, from which he had picked up float that assayed high in gold, but had not found it. She wanted me to take the property over under some kind of option, and try to locate that vein. But I do not care much for prospecting, and do not think I am much of a prospector. Besides, there is that resolve I made so many years ago not to try to do business with women, to which I have adhered so far as possible.

It might seem that, after so many years of intensive prospecting, and so many millions of dollars spent in mining, there are no new discoveries of ore to be made, but that is not true. Just the last few weeks, in an old gold-mining district in Mexico, about eighty-five miles from the Arizona line, there has been a fabulous discovery of placer gold, and there is a great rush on there, but "gringos" are strictly barred.

While I was at the mine in Arizona, a prospector and his son took over an old mine at Mojave, California, which had been abandoned many years ago, and I suppose, as most all such old mines, had been looked at by a thousand people to see if something worthwhile had not been overlooked. They sampled around in the old workings and discovered that a great vein of good gold ore was exposed there, apparently neglected in the belief that it was just country rock of no value. It was all ready for them to break it down and ship it to the smelter, which they proceeded to do and presently a big mining concern bought it from them for $3.5 million, put up a big mill, and have been working it ever since on a large scale.

My son is now mine superintendent on an old mine at Congress, Arizona, with a shaft 1,350 feet deep, abandoned forty or fifty years ago. I used to see the old dumps as I went by on the highway from Phoenix to Prescott, but never paid enough attention to it to find out what it was called or who owned it, although I examined a famous old abandoned mine adjoining it, which was offered me on a lease and option. A little over a year ago a man took it over, built a mill and started work, getting loans of $94,000 from the RFC. He has already paid up the loans, long before they were due, and the mine is doing very well. The people who originally worked this mine did not find pay ore until they got down more than six hundred feet.

The adjoining old mine that I looked at and did not want, was examined by engineers for a big mining concern just afterward, and turned down, as I suppose it had been at least a hundred times before. But after the price of gold went up, somebody took it over, built a mill, and has been working now for three or four years.

So I keep on looking, but not with very high hopes of success, as I am now seventy-six years old and getting quite deaf, which is quite a handicap; but I must do something to keep me occupied and to try and make a living while I wait, more or less impatiently, for the Grim Reaper, who is past due, to gather me in.[4]

THE AIMLESS LIFE.

This is the plain tale of the long life of an ordinary native American of average intelligence and education, without special talent or unusual opportunity, never rich, never in actual want, never holding any important position politically, economically or socially. Surely a drab and uninteresting recital, especially as the writer has neither literary talent nor experience, a commonplace person, with only commonplace thoughts and modes of expression. But most of our interest seems to center about the daily happenings of ourselves and our neighbors, and when we meet our talk is principally of such things. So who can tell, perhaps it may seem interesting to some. So I am going to write it anyhow, and if it interests no one there is no harm done. Perhaps as I progress practice may improve my style so that it may be come interesting.

My father was born in the Indian Territory in 1835, son of a Yankee missionary to the Cherokee Indians, who that same year established the first printing press in what is now Oklahoma. To complete his education my father was sent to the Academy at St. Johnsbury, Vt., where, during vacations, he worked in the scale factory of the Fairbanks Brothers and learned the machinist's trade. Then he married, and went to Van Buren, Arkansas, to teach music. But soon the Civil War started, and he took his wife to live with her mother in Dayton, Ky. until the war should be over.

My mother was born at Cincinnati, Ohio, the daughter of pioneer from New Hampshire, who came down the Ohio river on a flat-boat from Pittsburgh to Fort Washington, afterwards named Cincinnati, with their belongings aboard. Her father took up two homesteads, one Fort Washington, the other up the river a little way, on the Kentucky side, and he built the first brick house in Cincinnati, a two-story one on the river bank. My mother was born and grew up on the

4. Worcester as a toddler. Courtesy of Anne Worcester Coleman Rowe.

5. Worcester with the GAR Juvenile Drum Corps. Worcester had this studio portrait taken when he led the Drum Corps to Boston for the National Encampment in 1890. He mentions this photograph in this memoir's Coda. Courtesy of Anne Worcester Coleman Rowe.

6. Performers in Leadville. This image, taken in the late 1870s or 1880s, is likely that of the Blue Ribbon Comedy Club, where Leonard Worcester (*back row, third from left*) first met Gertrude Beede (*middle row, far right*), who would become his wife. Courtesy of Anne Worcester Coleman Rowe.

7. Amy Worcester. Born in Colorado in 1893, little Amy Worcester succumbed to typhoid three years later. Courtesy of Anne Worcester Coleman Rowe.

8. The Worcester family. This image was taken around 1905 and shows the Worcester family. *Left to right*: Arthur, Leonard, Barbara, Herbert, Gertrude, and Richard. Courtesy of Anne Worcester Coleman Rowe.

9. The Assay Office at the Hotel Palacio in Chihuahua. Worcester established a reputable and reliable business from the Hotel aPalacio in the center of the Ciudad de Chihuahua. Courtesy of Anne Worcester Coleman Rowe.

10. Leonard Worcester Jr. Courtesy of Anne Worcester Coleman Rowe.

11. Home in Chihuahua. Leonard, Barbara, and Gertrude Worcester stand at the back entrance to their home in Chihuahua. Courtesy of Anne Worcester Coleman Rowe.

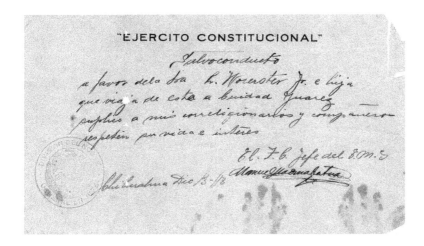

"EJERCITO CONSTITUCIONAL"

Salvoconducto a favor dela Sra. L. Worcester Jr. e hija que viaja de esta a Ciudad Juárez suplico a mis correligionarios y compañeros respeten su vida e interés

El. F. C. Jefe del 8.M.3

Chihuahua Dec 13-13 *Manuel Madinabeitia*

12. (*opposite top*) Father and daughter. Leonard Worcester reads the newspaper with his daughter, Barbara, at their home in Chihuahua around 1909. Courtesy of Anne Worcester Coleman Rowe.

13. (*opposite bottom*) At the piano. Because music was central to the Worcester family, Leonard, Gertrude, and Barbara spent much time at the piano. Courtesy of Anne Worcester Coleman Rowe.

14. (*above*) Salvoconducto. This note does not appear to be the one mentioned by Worcester in chapter 5, but it is a note of safe passage written by General Manuel Madinabeitia for "Mrs. Leonard Worcester Jr. and daughter" to travel from Chihuahua to Ciudad Juárez in December 1913. Documents like this give evidence of the danger of travel in the state in a time of revolution, but they also show how American capitalists relied on connections to (multiple) revolutionary factions to maintain operations. Courtesy of Anne Worcester Coleman Rowe.

15. Society life in Chihuahua. Gertrude Worcester (*second from right*) had a sizeable social circle among Americans in Chihuahua, most of whom knew James and Gertrude Eaton, Congregational missionaries with the American Board of Commissioners for Foreign Missions. This photo was taken between 1907 and 1910 at an Eaton garden party. Emily Eaton (*at center*), daughter-in-law of the missionaries, poses with her child. Courtesy of Anne Worcester Coleman Rowe.

16. (*opposite top*) A miner and assayer. Like many of his era, Leonard Worcester dressed formally, whether at the desk or in the mine. Courtesy of Anne Worcester Coleman Rowe.

17. (*opposite bottom*) In the field. Moses Beede (*left*) sits with Gertrude (his daughter) and Leonard Worcester, May 8, 1921. Courtesy of Anne Worcester Coleman Rowe.

18. (*opposite top*) Leonard and Gertrude Worcester.
Courtesy of Anne Worcester Coleman Rowe.

19. (*opposite bottom*) At Pike's Peak. The touring
couple likely stopped for this photograph. Courtesy
of Anne Worcester Coleman Rowe.

20. (*above*) Extended family and friends. The greater
Worcester family gathered for Christmastime in El
Paso in 1933. *From left to right:* son-in-law A. L. Holm,
Leonard, Gertrude, granddaughter Miriam, Peggy
and Bill Young (no relation), Cora Stevenson, son
Arthur, daughter-in-law Miriam, granddaughter
Barbara Jessie Holm Coleman, Walter Stockwell of El
Paso (no relation), Wilhelmina Stevenson Young (no
relation), and daughter Barbara Worcester Holm.

Notes

1. Worcester misremembers the year. He took the Leadville drum corps to Boston in 1890.

2. The Reconstruction Finance Corporation (RFC) assisted state and local governments with large-scale projects during the Great Depression.

3. Worcester's father-in-law was Moses Beede.

4. Worcester died on December 1, 1939, at his home in El Paso. Gertrude lived in El Paso for the remainder of her life, with the help of the family assistant, Marina. Gertrude passed away ten years later.

ACKNOWLEDGMENTS

THE PUBLICATION OF THIS MANUSCRIPT WOULD NOT HAVE been possible without the persistence of Anne Worcester Coleman Rowe. Anne did much more than provide her great-grandfather's manuscript. She scoured untold numbers of photographs, letters, and other materials in her family's possession to supplement *The Aimless Life*, and she fielded questions related to the life—and especially the broader family—of Leonard Worcester Jr. To these ends, she often peppered her mother, Barbara Holm Coleman, with questions at my request. Anne, a trained lawyer, also proofread the entire manuscript, providing ten single-spaced pages of comments and questions. She caught several errors and challenged interpretive points, thereby strengthening the finished product. To have a descendant committed to understanding the past as objectively as possible: what a luxury!

The William P. Clements Center for Southwest Studies at Southern Methodist University, where I held a postdoctoral fellowship in 2014–15, facilitated the transformation of this manuscript to a finished book. As always, it was a pleasure to work with the Center, and to count on the unwavering support of Andrew Graybill, Neil Foley, and Ruth Ann Elmore.

Miami University continues to be a superb home for a practicing historian. Conversations with many colleagues in the Department of History have contributed to these pages. In particular, Wietse de Boer provided guidance at key points in this project's development, and Elena Jackson Albarrán answered questions on

Mexican history and historiography. In the classroom, the university's emphasis on the teacher-scholar model helped me to gauge reception of *The Aimless Life*. Students in two offerings of my American West class read an unedited version of this memoir— straight from Worcester's fingertips and without my editing—to discuss exceptionalism, capitalism, and dispossession in the American West, along with more prosaic issues like the importance of paragraph breaks. In and beyond the classroom, Rich Bement's comments were especially helpful. Jacob Bruggeman assisted compiling Worcester's mine ledgers from 1928 to 1940. Mary Seaman, as an Undergraduate Summer Scholar, contributed research on Worcester's genealogy and migrations. Outside the Department of History, others affiliated with the Miami University Library were critical to my research, including University Archivist Jacqueline Johnson, Humanities and Social Sciences Librarian Jenny Presnell, and Sheila Sparks in the Interlibrary Loan Office.

A stellar team at the University of Nebraska Press—Bridget Barry, Matt Bokovoy, and Emily Wendell—acquired and produced this book and thereby, at long last, brought to light the words of Leonard Worcester Jr. Freelance cartographer Erin Greb produced the two excellent maps in this book.

Finally, a project such as this, completed during a pandemic, makes one reconsider and reevaluate the importance of family in personal and national history. Jeffrie Story, my mom, read aloud via FaceTime every page from the original manuscript to me, while I checked the finished product for fidelity to Worcester's words and intent. My other parents, Chuck and Carla Offenburger, visited (and quarantined) to play with their granddaughters while I slipped away for several hours to edit. At home in Oxford, my wife, María, and our three daughters—Audrey, Casey, and Lindsay— were remarkably patient and understanding as this project concluded during stay-at-home schooling. Daily life while social distancing felt without direction at times, and our home office became its own contested borderland. Inevitable challenges aside, these months at home with my family have been a gift. Indeed, perspective and purpose have flourished among aimlessness.

INDEX

Page numbers with f indicate illustrations

Burro Mountains, 119
burros, 23, 73, 112, 115
Bustillo Ranch, 78

Calderwood, John, 64n7
California Gulch, 43
Calles, Plutarco, 115–16
Cameron train station, 57
campesinos, 73, 89n9
Camp Grant Massacre, xx
cane, chewing, 7
Caraveo, Marcelo, 117–18, 124n26
Carlsbad Mountains, 127
Carothers, G. C., 122n7
Carranza, Venustiano, 84, 88, 111, 113; and
   American mine owners, 103; and Chihua-
   hua, 95, 103; as de-facto ruler, 103; fighting,
   101; government of, 122n10; and Woodrow
   Wilson, 102
Catalina Island
Catholics, 3
Cavender, Charles, 46, 64n3
Chase, Salmon P., 2
Cherokees, xi, xx, 1, 11n2
Cherokee Phoenix, 11n2
Chicago fire, 8
Chicago World's Columbian Exposition, 43
Chicago World's Fair, 64n2
Chickering, Elmer, 126
Chihuahua (city), F12, ix; and automobiles, 72;
   capture of, 82; Congregational church in,
   90n13; Federal buildings in, 85; Institute in,
   74; military bands in, 84; mine manager of,
   71; rental houses in, 75; society life in, F15;
   State Palace in, 85. *See also* Chihuahua (state)
Chihuahua (state): and Colorado-Chihuahua
   corridor, xx, 85; evacuating from, 85–86;
   mining region of, 96; and Porfirio Díaz vis-
   its, 75; refugees from, 107; selling mine in,
   76–77; as smelting center, 96; and zinc ores,
   68, 97. *See also* Agua Nueva, Mexico; Chihuahua State Government; Ciudad Juárez,
   Mexico; Cusihuiriachi, Mexico; Guerrero,
   Mexico; Jiménez, Mexico; Miñaca, Mexico; Ojinaga, Mexico; Parral, Mexico; Santa
   Eulalia, Mexico; Urique, Mexico
Chihuahua & Pacific Railroad, 69
Chihuahua Foreign Club, 116
Chihuahua State Government, 77
Christmas Day (1909), 60
church(es), xiii, xiv, xvi, 3, 11, 21, 53, 78, 115–
   16, 124n21

Chuviscar River, 96
Científicos, 79, 90n18
Citizens' Alliance, 61
Ciudad Juárez, Mexico, 78–79; attack on,
   90n17
Civil War (U.S.), 1
claims (mining), 62, 64n2, 122n11; in Arizona,
   129; "hay shovelers" and, 54; looking for, 36,
   55; selling, 36
Cleveland, Grover, 40n18
Climax Molybdenum Company, 125
Clydesdales, 31
cockfighting, 59
Cody, William F. "Buffalo Bill," 37n3
coining, 43, 95
Coleman, Barbara Holm. *See* Worcester, Bar-
   bara (daughter)
Colorado Midland line, 57
Colorado Mill Trust, 57
Colorado Mineral Resources Board, 19
Colorado National Guard, 49
Colorado School of Mines, 63; identifying
   dean of, 65n16
Colorado Springs CO, 54
Columbus NM, attack on, 108
Compañia Industrial, 94
Congregational church, 21, 53, 90n13
copper, 42, 51, 70, 93–94, 96, 119–20, 127
"Cousin Jacks" (Cornishmen), 27
Creede CO: boom in, 29, 40n17; silver in,
   40n17–18; and valley, 34
Creek Nation, xx, 4–5, 13n9
Creel, Enrique, 88n1
Cripple Creek CO, xii, xv, 48–51, 62, 125–
   27; fires at, 52–53, 65n9; camp and mine,
   52, 54–56, 61, 63; and Short Line, 57, 127;
   and Stock Exchange, 59; strike (1894), xii,
   64nn6–7, 65n14
Cumbre tunnel horror, 83–84, 91n28
Cusihuiriachi, mine at, 71, 103–4, 115, 122n11
Custer County Chief (newspaper), 38n6
Custer County NE, 38n6

D.&R.G. Railroad. *See* Denver & Rio Grande
   Railroad (D.&R.G.)
Day, James M., xxi
Dayton KY: living in, 7; men living in, 4
Defensa Social, 110–12, 123n19
Del Norte CO, 30
Denver & Rio Grande Railroad (D.&R.G.),
   30, 57
Denver CO, 26, 30, 34, 36, 61, 114, 127; form-

CPSIA information can be obtained
at www.ICGtesting.com
Printed in the USA
LVHW031955190521
687902LV00005B/279

9 781496 222909